Teaching Genius

Redefining Education with Lessons from Science and Philosophy

Chris Edwards

Rowman & Littlefield Education
A division of
ROWMAN & LITTLEFIELD PUBLISHERS, INC.
Lanham • Boulder • New York • Toronto • Plymouth, UK

Thomas

Published by Rowman & Littlefield Education
A division of Rowman & Littlefield Publishers, Inc.
A wholly owned subsidiary of
The Rowman & Littlefield Publishing Group, Inc.
4501 Forbes Boulevard, Suite 200, Lanham, Maryland 20706
http://www.rowmaneducation.com

Estover Road, Plymouth PL6 7PY, United Kingdom

British Library Cataloguing in Publication Information Available

Library of Congress Cataloging-in-Publication Data

Edwards, Chris, 1977-
Teaching genius : redefining education with lessons from science and philosophy / Chris Edwards.
p. cm.
Includes bibliographical references.
ISBN 978-1-61048-815-0 (cloth : alk. paper) -- ISBN 978-1-61048-816-7 (pbk. : alk. paper) -- ISBN
978-1-61048-817-4 (ebook)
1. Teaching--Philosophy. 2. Education--Aims and objectives. I. Title.
LB1025.3.E345 2012
371.102--dc23
2012010451

The paper used in this publication meets the minimum requirements of American National
Standard for Information Sciences Permanence of Paper for Printed Library Materials,
ANSI/NISO Z39.48-1992.

Printed in the United States of America

For Dr. Joel Boaz, a great surgeon and humanitarian, who embodies the spirit of Riley Hospital for Children. For D. Chie-Schin Shih and his pediatric oncology staff at Riley. For Dr. Jeffrey Buchsbaum and his radiation oncology team in Bloomington, Indiana. Your combined dedication, professionalism, and genius saved Ben and others like him.

Contents

Preface: Joining the Left and Right Hands of Education   vii

Acknowledgments   xiii

**Part I: Lessons for Education from the History and Philosophy
of Science**   **1**

1   Defining Teaching as a Field   5

2   Content Area Professional Development   11

3   Educating Consilience   21

4   Neuroscience and Consilience   27

5   Applications for Principals and Education Professors   35

6   Applications for Various Academic Disciplines   41

Part II: Connecting the Dots   **47**

7   Lesson One: Human Migration   55

8   Lesson Two: Assessment for Historical Pattern Recognition   65

9   Lesson Three: Historical Paradigm Shift   67

10   Lesson Four: Caffeine and Connections—A Tempest in a
Coffeepot   93

11   Lesson Five: Applications of Insights to a Historical
Narrative   109

Conclusion: A Vision for the Future   119

References   121

About the Author   125

Preface: Joining the Left and Right Hands of Education

I have never let my schooling interfere with my education. —Mark Twain

I don't know anything about music. In my line of work I don't have to. —Elvis Presley

When motivated former students come to speak to me about their college plans, I often give them the same speech about needing to have a right and a left hand to their education. The right hand of education involves leaping from one academic requirement to another in order to gain credibility and the honors that come from completing a formal academic program. The left hand of education is less specific and bureaucratic, more like falling in love, and involves the study of content for the purpose of individual discovery and the passion of understanding.

I am still convinced that this speech presents good advice, although it is a little depressing. Ideally, the right and left hands would be joined and the process of passionate inquiry and study molded into a formalized system. Good teachers do this; they make the right and left hands fold together on a daily basis.

Unfortunately, much of educational policy and practice remains based upon a false notion of what education should be. Education should be guided by the right concepts and metaphors, by the idea of education as a performance. To explain what I mean, imagine you are given the task of teaching a typing class and are told that, in six months, the students will be given a typing exam that will test their abilities. So you have your students put their fingers on the keyboard and type, practicing every day until new neurons dig their canals into the brain and until the fingers become educated.

Now, imagine that on the day of the assessment the students are given a test asking them where each letter is on the keyboard. Every student would fail because you had trained them for performance, whereas the assessment tested for a different type of thought. (If you fancy yourself a competent typist, try this test yourself and see how far beyond QWERTY you get.)

Clearly, passing the keyboard location test would not mean that one could actually type any more than being able to describe the types of strings on a violin would indicate the ability to play a virtuoso piece. This is not to denigrate the right hand of education; where would we be without formalized training practices in law or medicine, for example?

Universities must establish standards for accreditation, and the professions necessarily standardize licensure requirements. However, deep education requires an individual initiative to study beyond the curriculum, a passion for content that cannot be inculcated by official programs. About ten years ago, I developed the beneficial habit of rising early every day to read while sipping two cups of coffee. This content area study has informed and improved my teaching far more than the formal process that was necessary to accrue university degrees and licensure.

Through this process of daily study, concepts and connections made themselves apparent. It became possible for me to see patterns in the information, to construct timelines, and answer large-scale structural questions about knowledge and its meanings. Seeing these concepts created a desire to share the connections with others. Obviously, I had chosen the right profession, as my job entailed my sharing of these insights with students.

How to do this? It was one thing to read through often thick tomes on history or science or philosophy and understand concepts for myself, but making these concepts accessible to teenagers added an additional, seemingly insurmountable, obstacle.

Sure, this would be difficult, I reasoned, but from where did this concept that education was easy come from? No one expects that chess grandmasters, or excellent violin players, or high level neurosurgeons, or paradigm-busting philosophers and scientists have come by their insights and talents easily.

If I had learned a lot from reading and thinking in such a free-form way, then it was my duty to try to recreate those conditions for my students. I embraced the notion that I was not a game show host, nor an entertainer, but an educator.

Using essay writing and reading comprehension lessons, students gain time to practice skills such as reading, comprehension, and the ability to articulate the connections they see and the concepts they develop. This is the actual work of history and the process of thinking historically and philosophically. Why waste time with anything else?

Working from the concept that my job as a teacher was to act as a bridge between the scholarship being created by academics and the classroom, I developed a teaching method called "Connecting the Dots." One lesson, later published by the National Council for Social Studies, highlighted each of the concepts in Jared Diamond's book *Guns, Germs, and Steel* by presenting the students with a historical question, followed by the evidence needed to answer the question.

To assess learning, students had to apply what they had discovered to a quote they had not seen and articulate their answer through essay writing. Such a lesson required students to improve reading comprehension skills, analyze documents, think in a historical way, and, finally, to apply their learning to a piece of evidence that they had not yet seen. The entire lesson flowed from and was dependent on my own level of content area mastery as a teacher.

Guided by this notion, my reading became active, as each book was read with an eye toward creating lessons from the content. Whenever I read a passage of scholarship that was relevant to my standards, I would copy it down, incorporate it into the method's system, and present it to my students.

This intense intellectual work proved to be addictive, as I could not imagine beginning the day with an ordinary lesson plan, one not designed to present the students with some concept or connection that was sure to provoke deep thought and study.

Eventually, this Frankenstein's document cobbled together from different sources totaled about 1200 pages. I divided the document into sections, had it copied, and then distributed it *samizdat* style to the students. This was my way of saying "I've read a lot of books, found some interesting questions and patterns, and now let's see if you can find them too." If teachers are to invite students to see bigger-picture concepts, then teachers have to see them first.

A goal of mine, for a very long time, was to formalize the "connect-the-dots" method into a textbook with the hope of presenting it to teachers as a complete system of ideas. Eventually, the illogical thinking behind such a goal became apparent. The last thing that education needs is another complete system. Anecdotal evidence and my own experience have showed me that teachers resent the condescending notion that we exist solely to incorporate the ideas of people outside of the classroom.

Instead of a system, a good educational philosophy acts like a greenhouse, providing the right conditions for ideas to grow. This book represents an argument and an invitation for teachers to rethink their profession and for administrators to rethink how they view their teachers. Teacher education, and the concept of teaching, can be altered if teachers conceive of themselves as practitioners in a field of inquiry, one which will require a lifetime of intensive study followed by classroom application.

This book consists of two parts. The first part contains a series of arguments from the fields of the history and philosophy of science, neuroscience, and education. The purpose of these arguments is to redefine the field of teaching in such a way that the reforms are being made and engaged in "behind the classroom door," rather than imposed from outside the door.

Teachers can embrace these concepts personally and immediately and use the arguments here to inform daily practice. A chapter for administrators spells out possible applications for the development of school culture and professional development activities in the arguments presented here.

A compendium of lesson plans makes up the second part and is intended to showcase the "connect-the-dots" curriculum, a synthesis of methods and content, as a coherent and organic system that is the practical and useful manifestation of the philosophy argued for in the first part. (Incidentally, this concept of teaching also influenced me in other ways, as I began to write and publish on historical, philosophical, and scientific concepts for various peer-reviewed journals.)

Contributing to the world of ideas through publication has long been a staple of the academic, medical, and legal professions; there is no reason why secondary teachers should not be seen as intellectual contributors in this vein. Teachers who publish help bring legitimacy to the field.

Through my study and writing on theoretical physics, I discovered that scientists and philosophers engage in the same type of intellectual process that teachers do. For example, theoretical physicists take complex concepts and try to understand them using various metaphors, analogies, and scientific systems. Teachers, too, take complicated ideas and make them understandable to students. My own work in philosophy and theoretical physics stems directly from my engagement in classroom teaching.

In one peer-reviewed science and philosophy journal (I state this not to brag, but to note that the idea has been vetted, which separates it from the many entries on theoretical physics which dot the blogosphere), I wrote on the topic of model-dependent realism (MDR), which was a term coined by Stephen Hawking and Leonard Mlodinow in their book *The Grand Design*. In that article (and elsewhere), I argued that a theoretical position called M-theory (more or less the combination of the five different types of string theory) really should be called L-theory, which stands for Language.

Model-dependent realism treats mathematical and scientific theories about the universe as if they were languages. Languages cannot be right or wrong, but are, rather, more or less descriptive. The challenge of science and theoretical physics, then, is to create theories and models that are the most descriptive of the behavior of the universe and the particles within it.

The application of this analogy can be admittedly a bit weird. The way to test theories or models, according to MDR, is to see which approach works best for whatever the phenomena and then to choose among the models. As we attempt to understand the universe around us, we are engaged in a process of creating models that are more or less descriptive and useful. Education across wide fields trains the mind to find patternicity among facts and to create analogies, metaphors, and models that may turn out to be useful in uniting or advancing disciplines.

Model-dependent realism, as an epistemological position, creates an exciting time for young thinkers and theorists, but they have to be educated properly. Many of the ideas argued for in the following pages are informed by MDR as future thinkers will need a certain mental agility and a particular kind of intellectual training if progress is to be made in the sciences—and if this is to occur, they need to be trained by teachers who possess the same type of thought process.

At the moment, MDR can be described as "pure philosophy" in the same way that mathematicians sometimes refer to esoteric and abstract mathematics at very high levels as "pure mathematics." History, however, provides any number of examples of how pure mathematics eventually yields stunning breakthroughs in applied mathematics, or mathematics that can be useful in an everyday way.

To use but two examples: The Hellenistic genius Archimedes created the mathematical techniques necessary to represent a round surface on a flat surface. Archimedes was just having fun, but when his theorems were rediscovered during the Renaissance, they made it possible to make maps for navigation, which was one of the more important technological developments of an era exploding with novel devices and concepts.

Likewise, Gottfried Liebniz, a Baroque-era genius and contemporary of Isaac Newton, invented a new numbering system made of nothing but zeroes and ones. This brilliant system sat collecting dust for a little more than two hundred years because it required too much memory for humans to use—but when the computer evolved, Liebniz's binary code became the language of the Information Revolution.

Less concrete, but equally as important, were the revolutions of thought propagated by Newton, Darwin, and Einstein. These men began what Thomas Kuhn would call "scientific paradigm shifts," and, by setting the epistemological and theoretical boundaries for their disciplines, created an atmosphere in which other thinkers could flourish and see further. No one knows what practical implications MDR will have as a future position, but teaching students to think under its theoretical umbrella may prove fruitful.

I teach history, so the lessons come from that discipline, which I consider to be a nexus point for all academic disciplines. However, I do not want to disparage the expertise of my colleagues in other fields by attempting to create lesson plans in areas of teaching that I am not an expert in. Readers of Part II, which includes practical application, should not get too enmeshed in the actual form of the lessons, but rather try to determine the philosophy behind them and use that as a guide for their own disciplines and classes.

The purpose of the curriculum is to allow for teachers to continually engage and reshape it as they go, to excite teachers to contribute, not to coerce them into implementation. This, more than anything, is the intellectual shift I hope this book facilitates.

Two points about the layout of the text: First, much of this book draws on wisdom from past thinkers. Rather than try to work large chunks of the work of past philosophers into the text, I've chosen to quote them at the beginning of the chapters for the most part. This is a somewhat unusual use of quotes, but I wanted to give credit to past philosophers and also invite readers to see that the ideas presented here are rooted in the history of thought. Second, the "key points" at the end of the chapters may appear a bit repetitive if read immediately after a chapter's completion. My hope, however, is that this book will be a continual resource for teachers as they guide their daily work and I know how useful a summary of key ideas can be for a teacher in a hurry.

Acknowledgments

To begin, please let me thank my kind and patient editors at Rowman & Littlefield Education, Dr. Tom Koerner and Mary McMenamin, for their guidance. Dr. Michael Shermer, editor of *Skeptic* magazine, deserves my great appreciation for making suggestions on the essay (which he published) upon which this book is constructed.

Thanks to my mom and dad for their assistance in my education.

Thanks also to the staff at Fishers High School, where I teach and have the freedom to experiment in the classroom with new ideas.

Thanks to Dr. Charles Guthrie who helped start me on this journey. Thanks also to Dr. Carol Rubel for her kind assistance on my doctoral work, upon much of which this is book is based. Chaz Bufe also deserves my appreciation for his patient editorial advice.

Special thanks go to my wife, Beth, who almost never distracts me when I am writing, and to my sons Ben and Blake, who almost always do.

Part I

Lessons for Education from the History and Philosophy of Science

[T]he need for new methods in fact only arises in circumstances that give rise to new methods. . . . —Marquis de Condorcet, 1794

[T]ruths that were discovered only by great effort, that could at first be understood by men capable of profound thought, are soon developed and proved by methods that are not beyond the reach of common intelligence. If the methods which have led to these new combinations of ideas are ever exhausted . . . some method of a greater generality or simplicity will be found so that genius can continue undisturbed on its path. The strength and limits of man's intelligence may remain unaltered; and yet the instruments he uses will increase and improve, the language that fixes and determines his ideas will acquire greater breadth and precision. . . . —Marquis de Condorcet, 1794

Teachers are the most important school-based factor for affecting student achievement. Large-scale political initiatives to change education, whether they come in the form of managerial techniques, charter school schemes, private school voucher programs, or professional development configurations, often are defeated by the simplest of technologies: the classroom door.

Teachers choose, to a large extent, which ideas will make it through the door and which will not. This book was written with the understanding that educational improvement begins with teacher improvement and that lessons taken from the field of history and philosophy of science can shape current educational policy and professional development.

Most forms of bad thinking, and thus bad policy, have at their core a false metaphor or analogy. The bad analogy in education has been to assume that schools are like businesses, teachers are like executives, parents are like shareholders, principals are like CEOs, and test scores are like stock dividends. Under this simplistic reasoning, one need merely to treat the teachers as executives: "Fire the bad teachers, and pay the good teachers more."

All too often, this business-as-education analogy leads to disastrous results. Serious and widespread cheating allegations in Texas, Atlanta, and Washington, D.C., show that when schools are treated like corporations, the staff can fudge the numbers as well as Enron. Under the business model, teachers are often treated as individuals to be forced or flattered into swallowing curricular programs developed by individuals outside the classroom.

In logical reasoning, a common error involves the confusion of an abstract concept with an actual material thing and is known as *reification*. In education, the fallacy most often committed in the modern era is *Rheeification*, named after the former D.C. schools' superintendent and educational "reformer" Michelle Rhee. Rheeification occurs when someone mistakes a coercive management style for an educational philosophy.

This is not to bash all educational reform methods (although some bashing is warranted); it is merely to state that good teaching is good teaching, and whether it occurs in a private, public, or charter school classroom is of little significance. Educational reform philosophies should be informed by lessons taken from the history of ideas, discovery, and intellectual revolution. The history and philosophy of science is a field that offers much richer lessons for teachers than the comparatively shallow field of business management.

Teachers will shape educational reform. This simple and obvious fact should guide all reform efforts. Administrators play a definite and important role, but teachers are the individuals who guide students and have the ultimate educational impact on the people in their charge.

KEY POINTS

- Teachers are the most important school-based factor for determining student achievement levels. Teachers are responsible for enacting curricular changes in the classroom and may choose to implement reforms or not. Therefore, philosophies of education looking to affect change should take the form of logical arguments made to teachers in such a way that is respectful of their ambition and talents. Student improvement must be preceded by teacher improvement.

- Recent educational reform efforts have been built upon analogies taken from the field of business management. The field of history and philosophy of science, which provides a deep well of metaphors about ideas, the brain, and methods of scholarship, provides more lessons for informing curricular change at the classroom practice level.

- New developments in philosophy and theoretical physics have created an epistemological and metaphysical framework that puts a high priority on creative thinking for the development of descriptive metaphors, analogies, and models. This type of philosophical thinking, while still at the phase of "pure philosophy" will, if history is any guide, eventually yield impressive practical applications.

ONE

Defining Teaching as a Field

It is idle to expect any great advancement in science from the superinducing and engrafting of new things upon old. We must begin anew from the very foundations, unless we would revolve forever in a circle with mean and contemptible progress. —Francis Bacon, 1620

A complaint often heard from teachers (besides the obvious one about starting salary) involves the lack of respect afforded to teachers. The public holds other professions, such as law, higher education, and medicine, in higher esteem. There are no equivalents, for example, to the condescending Teach for America (where graduates from respected universities teach for two years after graduation as a kind of charity work, or as a favor to the profession) in medicine. What is it, then, that separates teaching from these other endeavors? The answer is that teachers are not seen as practitioners in a field.

Doctors involved in the medical profession not only practice medicine in a practical everyday way but typically involve themselves in research studies, publishing results of their inquiries and treatments to advance the field. Lawyers also find publication to be a vital component of the profession, as well as necessary for advancement. The pressures on academics to achieve publication are well known (and occasionally lamented).

Teachers, however, face no such expectation. Tell someone you are a teacher and she is much more likely to ask you what team you coach or club you sponsor than to ask in what journal you publish. This must change if teaching is to gain greater acceptance as an intellectually challenging and respectable profession, a change that is necessary to attract bright young people into the classroom.

The first step to changing the perception of teaching is to define it as a field with clear parameters and then to encourage the teachers themselves to shape that field.

The history and philosophy of science provides a deep well of analogies, metaphors, and guiding principles for educational theory. One of the most important guiding principles to be gained from the sciences is how invigorating a new field can be if it provides not a coercive system, but a framework for allowing others to participate in the creation of new knowledge. Great things occurred in the sciences, in philosophy, and in academia once these fields became organic and allowed for the participants to shape and grow their respective fields.

Francis Bacon (1561–1626) published his treatise *Novum Organum* (New Method) in 1620. In this book, Bacon questioned the late medieval intellectual world's practice of assuming that knowledge of the world was more or less complete. This knowledge system, then based upon the intellectually rich traditions of Greek philosophy, had been the basis of Western university education for centuries. However, since the 13th century, when the Parisian monk and scholar St. Thomas Aquinas had melded Aristotle's logic (newly discovered by Western Christians via the Islamic world) with Christianity, the enterprise of critical and creative thinking had stagnated.

Bacon did not disparage Aristotle; indeed, to do so would be to perjure one of the greatest practitioners of critical thought in the history of philosophy. Instead, Bacon encouraged his readers to *study* Aristotle, but he cautioned them against worshipping ancient thinkers. The point of the intellectual and academic enterprise, according to Bacon, is to build upon what has been previously known.

It naturally follows, to a natural philosopher like Bacon, that knowledge is gathered and compiled through the process of experiment. The knowledge that resulted from these experiments would be stored in an early ancestor of the modern database, which Bacon called the *table of discovery*. By stating this philosophy, Bacon did not create a system of thought to be imposed upon his readers. Instead, he acknowledged the importance of previous sources of knowledge, but implored others to engage, not in the rote memorization of previous findings, but in the *process* of inquiry and thought that creates insights.

This same type of philosophical change occurred in the universities of Germany as the 18th century began. Prior to this era, the secular university (the offspring of the Christian monasteries, which were the only centers of learning in medieval Europe) concerned itself primarily with passing on the wisdom of the ancients. Peter Watson, the historian of ideas, wrote that "The norm was the teaching of static truths, not new ideas; professors were not expected to produce new knowledge. . . . " (2010, p. 50). At the universities of Halle—particularly at Gottingen—the concept of the teacher radically shifted, with professors now expected to be practitioners—that is, people who were actively engaged in the expansion of a field of knowledge.

This change in the definition of what it meant to be a teacher spawned several exciting innovations. The first of these, Watson noted, was the introduction of the professional journal. Scholars engaged in the meaningful work of refining a field and pushing its boundaries needed a means by which to share their findings and creativity with colleagues. Of course, those colleagues were the people in the best position to judge the fitness of these new ideas, so that the act of peer review and the prestige of being published served to refine and facilitate the furtherance of the new fields of inquiry.

An alteration of what it meant to be a teacher facilitated a change in what it meant to be a student. After all, if teachers are best trained and developed by pushing the frontiers of their disciplines, isn't it reasonable to assume that the same process would be solid intellectual training for the students? Watson wrote:

> Gottingen also developed and refined the seminar. This was another innovation whose importance it is difficult to exaggerate. The seminar, as we shall see, led to the modern concept of research, to the modern Ph.D., to the academic and scientific "disciplines" or subjects, and to the modern organization of universities into "departments," divided equally between teaching and research. (p. 52)

The result of these academic changes was a massive leap forward in virtually every field of intellectual endeavor, what Watson called a "second scientific revolution" in Germany. Further revolutions followed in Britain and the United States, where the German university model was replicated. This mode has been so successful that it remains the status quo at every major university in the Western world.

Secondary teaching has not embraced the notion that teachers, in addition to being engaged in traditional classroom practice, should also be involved in pushing forward a field. Nothing has been more toxic to the profession's prestige, to its ability to attract and keep new practitioners, or to classroom application than this stunning omission. *Teaching is currently not a field.*

Teachers are not asked to engage in the development of a body of knowledge in addition to being classroom practitioners. There are two reasons for this. The first is that the teacher-as-researcher model, developed over two hundred years ago, does not fit well with classroom teachers. Teachers are too busy to research primary documents and the like for publication in academic journals, so that the idea of a history teacher (for example) taking the time to research and publish new work on, say, the Civil War, is simply inapplicable and impractical.

Second, teaching is not seen as a separate field from education, defined here as the development of methods (defined broadly as classroom

curriculum, management programs, and teacher professional development) and the act of researching the efficacy of those methods. Thus,
teachers have become a population to be convinced or coerced into
adopting educational techniques developed by others invested in educational management techniques. Educational reformers are all too often
engaged in work that is vastly different from that of classroom teaching.

In fact, teaching has never fit easily inside either the research discipline model or the education model. Teachers are not researchers, nor are
we concerned solely with methods (as education is). Teaching must be
defined as a separate field of endeavor, and the definition I propose,
which forms the syllogistic base for the rest of the argument in this book
is this: *Teaching involves the application of methods to research-based content
for the purpose of opening minds and educating students.*

If the field of teaching is defined as the application of methods to
content for the purpose of educating students, then the work of teaching
involves bridging the gap between university research and the secondary
classroom. In other words, it is the job of a teacher to delve deeply into
the best scholarship in a content area and then apply methods training to
conceive ways in which to make that content understandable to students.
This is intense intellectual work.

Yet, there are no academic journals devoted to the field of teaching as
defined here, no collection of a body of work in which teachers can write
about how they applied methods training to specific forms of content
(books, articles, etc.) to make that content applicable to the secondary
classroom.

Making teaching a field would involve something much deeper than
sharing lesson plans. It would define the teacher as an individual whose
job it is to immerse herself in the study of particular content. It would
redefine the role and training of the individual educator as being one in
which the educator bridges the gap between academia and the classroom.
This redefinition would lead to refinements in professional development
and in the university training of teachers.

KEY POINTS

- Good philosophical constructs, like those developed by Francis Bacon, work like greenhouses in that they provide the right conditions for ideas to grow. Teachers should not be viewed as individuals who adopt systems and methods, but as professionals who are
  invited to shape and advance their field even as they engage in
  practical day-to-day application.
- The history of the university system provides an important lesson
  for modern secondary education. In the 18th century, the German
  Universities of Halle and Gottingen invented the teacher-as-re-

searcher concept, which encouraged teachers to be creators of new knowledge, as well as transmitters of old knowledge. This concept invigorated the various academic fields, as the process of engaging in research enriched the teachers and, thus, their methods and instruction.

- The time-consuming work of teaching secondary school means that high school teachers cannot realistically work as researchers. However, teaching can be defined as a field separate from education. The field of teaching, defined here, involves the application of methods to specific forms of content for the purpose of making content accessible to secondary students.
- Potential future ideas for teaching would involve the development of academic journals devoted to the compilation of methods by which teachers have bridged the distance between new forms of scholarship and the classroom. This would allow for teachers to use their creativity and intelligence to add to a field while also providing a database of accessible ideas for potential classroom use.

TWO

Content Area Professional Development

Without exception, outstanding teachers knew their subjects extremely well. They are all active and accomplished scholars, artists, or scientists. Some have long and impressive publication lists, the kind the academy has long valued. Others have more modest records; or in a few cases, virtually none at all. But whether well published or not, the outstanding teachers follow the important intellectual and scientific or artistic developments within their fields, do research, have important and original thoughts on their subjects, study carefully and extensively what other people are doing in their fields, often read extensively in other fields (sometimes far distant from their own), and take a strong interest in the broader issues of their disciplines: the histories, controversies, and epistemological discussions. In short, they can do intellectually, physically, or emotionally what they expect from their students. —Ken Bain, 2004

Much of this book argues for a shift in the perception of what teaching is and an alteration of the notion of what kind of work in which teachers are involved. One must be very cautious, in education, when putting forth ideas about actual structural changes. The machinery of education is complex, and professional development activities often must be tailored to meet specific legal needs or the expectations of local administrative teams.

With this caveat stated, the logical extension of the philosophy of education stated here would be to include structural changes to teacher professional development that would emphasize content area study. School districts that allowed for at least a portion of professional development time to be allocated to the study of content would take seriously those researchers who indicate that content area mastery is an integral part of teacher effectiveness.

Admittedly, the time allocated for professional development would not be sufficient to create deep content area knowledge in a teacher's subject. Content study during professional development time would, however, indicate to teachers that the administration took them seriously as scholars in a field. It would also establish expectations that content area study is an important part of teacher development. Some pretty good lesson plans might also be a result.

The major conceit of this book is that teacher training should be an ongoing process—throughout the teacher's life—of study, discovery, and implementation of discovery into the classroom. Much of this involves the "left-handed" learning described in the preface, but, wherever possible, school districts can and should encourage such a notion through formal professional development activities. To that end, the following arguments and possible forms of implementation are offered.

To restate an earlier point, researchers have consistently found that the individual classroom teacher is the most important school-based factor for affecting student performance. Many school reformers have decided that, based on these findings, the way to boost student performance is simply to use the old "carrot-and-stick" routine on teachers, by firing the worst and giving bonus pay to the best.

Such simplistic reasoning does little to address the deeper questions involving school reform. Instead, findings about the importance of individual teachers should renew interest in research and discussion about what can be done to properly attract, keep, and train effective teachers.

Inquiries into teacher effectiveness have revealed that certain teacher qualities are good predictors of classroom effectiveness. Several studies have indicated that teachers who score highly on verbal tests tend to have students who score higher on standardized tests. More significantly, research done on the topic of teacher content knowledge has found that a teacher's level of content area mastery may be the single most important form of knowledge that he or she can have.

One researcher, Benjamin Bain, saw a clear place for content area instruction for world history teachers and stated "Deep knowledge of world history makes a difference as teachers cannot teach well what they do not know well" (2004, p. 34). In addition, Bain noted that teachers with strong content mastery can see bigger-picture concepts that can then be transmitted to students.

This latter point raises an interesting question: Is content area knowledge more important for the teacher than it is for the students? Every teacher knows that there are limits to how much factual knowledge can be transmitted in the course of a school year. Ineffective history teachers try to get students to memorize as many facts as possible, which are usually quickly forgotten after the test concludes.

Effective history teachers focus instead on building up writing skills, patterns of thought, and the ability to create factually based arguments.

This can be achieved by teaching history through the prism of historiography. However, *the teacher* has to know the facts before he or she can plot a meaningful path through them. To emphasize Bain's earlier point, a teacher can't teach what he or she does not know.

Good teaching has a scholarly, contemplative side. The universities (perhaps before budget concerns and big-time athletics twisted the priorities of those who run them) have long embraced the idea that professors need time to study their content. The 18th-century shift in the German universities, summarized in the preceding chapter, grew from the philosophy that teacher preparation equaled student achievement.

Yet, the secondary teacher too often finds herself teaching three different subjects, coaching a team, sponsoring a club, and taking graduate-level courses paid for out of her own pocket. The culture of secondary education simply does not promote the creation of deep content area study among teachers.

Unfortunately, a lack of content area knowledge typically leaves a teacher, particularly a new teacher, reliant on the textbook and workbook materials presented by textbook companies. History textbooks, in particular, have come under serious criticism in the last few decades from both leftist and rightist historians, not only for factual inaccuracies but for a bland presentation of history that lacks the guiding thesis that historiography provides.

If teachers are not in a university environment, two options remain for them to update their content area knowledge. Teachers can study content on their own, or they can do so through formal professional development activities. Teachers who embrace the concept of teaching spelled out here need not wait for their schools to offer content area professional development.

However, administrators and teacher leaders interested in professional development might find it beneficial to create a school culture that embraces the study of content area knowledge. This is done elsewhere; in Finland, where in 2011 the schools were ranked best in the world by *Newsweek* magazine, teachers are expected to carry master's degrees both in education and the content area they instructed (Darling-Hammond 2010). In Finland, ongoing professional development activities included regular time to contemplate lessons and work with colleagues.

This is a bit of a side point, but worth stating. A teacher who embraces the philosophy of education detailed here may find himself more engaged and less likely to experience burnout. (No studies have been conducted on the effects of content area professional development on teacher retention.) Researchers should try to find out what engages teachers because experience affects teacher effectiveness, and teachers often leave the field before their skills peak.

There is a significant need to revamp professional development in order to train and excite highly qualified classroom teachers. Researchers indicate that engaging forms of professional development can have a positive effect on teacher retention.

The role of administrators who embrace this philosophy would be to create a school culture in which content area study and mastery is prized and in which content area study becomes a part of ongoing professional development. Teaching involves the application of methods to content, and yet the study of content rarely makes up any part of professional development activities.

Teachers, however, can study content on their own and engage in the process of making themselves content area masters—and thus better teachers. A potential criticism of this notion is that teachers do not have the time to study content. Yet, teachers routinely coach, tutor, or take on club sponsorship roles because these activities are good for students. Taking time to study content is one of the most important things a teacher can do for his students. Teachers must understand that the act of enhancing ourselves enhances our students by proxy.

WHAT SHOULD CONTENT AREA PROFESSIONAL DEVELOPMENT LOOK LIKE?

If professional development is to have a significant impact on enhancing teacher knowledge—and eventually improve student outcomes—then it stands to reason that districts providing professional development should include this focus within their professional development programs. Anyone seeking to develop a type of professional development that focuses on content should consult the research before proposing the shape and structure of that professional development.

In this case, the literature review focuses on the best techniques in professional development and techniques in andragogy (adult learning). Content area professional development would require teachers to learn specific types of content and thus differs from traditional professional development activities, hence the need to shape professional development activities around adult learning styles.

To begin, learning has to be seen as a fluid process, intimately related to living itself. Philosophers and educators have been interested in adult education for centuries, going back at least to Rousseau, who saw nature as being a pure guide to self-reflection. John Dewey argued that learning is something that comes from lifelong experience.

Modern research shows that the most effective forms of adult education adhere to five basic principles. Adults learn when they (1) are not under a threat; (2) are treated as colleagues; (3) have developed their own learning style; (4) are allowed to progress at their own pace, depending upon their educational background; and (5) when the education is tailored to their physical situation. Effective forms of adult education involving teachers should include both individual and collective features and should focus on improving the cognitive skills of teachers, who can then pass those skills on to students.

There is a growing consensus about how professional development should be structured. Cooperation between teachers and administrators is a must. As will be argued in chapter 5, one of the greatest differences between failing and improving schools is that, in failing schools, a greater gap exists between the teachers and administration. Several researchers call for schools to tear down hierarchies and provide opportunities for teacher leadership.

The specific implementation of content area professional development should be shaped by the teachers involved. Treating teachers as content area masters means letting them have some control over what content they think is worth studying and the way in which that content will be studied and, finally, implemented in the classroom.

Each school has different structural dynamics involving daily schedules, time set aside for professional development, and limits for the teacher work day. Likewise, each department or cohort contains different personalities and levels of collegiality. There is no one-size-fits-all method to any type of professional development, and that is equally true of content area professional development. The following forms of content area professional development are merely suggestions that were created to be in alignment with the previously noted research on professional development and andragogy.

DESIGN 1: THE BOOK CLUB

Teachers in various contents might find a book club approach to content area professional development to be a good first step. Given the time constraints that most schools deal with, teachers who choose such an option would likely have to agree to read a content area book outside of the school day. Teachers of social studies, for example, could choose to divide up a book on the topic of history or psychology over the course of a semester or a year and agree to read a certain number of chapters before each meeting.

Discussion of the selected books should be guided by specific educational questions that allow teachers to manipulate content in a way that is meaningful to their students. Guiding questions should be simple, such as: "How can I bring this content into my classroom?" Sub-questions should involve specifics, and teachers should be invited to share how they plan to incorporate, using their methods training, the newly learned scholarship into daily lessons.

The first meetings of the book club would involve possibilities for bringing the scholarship into the classroom, while later meetings would involve teachers discussing the specific methods they used to get scholarship into the classroom, while also planning future lessons. Such cognitive manipulation enhances a teacher's understanding of the content.

Teachers of other subjects, such as math, science, or English, might find any number of books about statistics, randomness, literary criticism, or the history and philosophy of science to be of interest to them. They may find novel connections or be introduced to new concepts that they could then work to bring into the classroom.

DESIGN 2: ARTICLE CLUB

Not every teacher will be willing or able to read a full-length book in his or her spare time, and many teacher contracts would prohibit such a book club design from being made an administrative directive. However, even schools with limited time for professional development could implement a shortened version of the book club that would not violate teacher contracts. If teachers were allotted a forty-five-minute period for professional development, then an article from a scholarly journal in the field could be read for the first half of that time period, and discussion and collaboration could occur during the second half.

In a given year, this approach could expose teachers to several different articles in their field. This would allow for teachers to be kept abreast of new scholarship, while at the same time challenging them to find innovative ways to get new information into the classroom and making them feel as if they are a part of an intellectual community that includes researchers and professors.

DESIGN 3: DOCUMENTARY STUDY

Reading is obviously not the only way in which teachers can become exposed to information in their fields. Teachers may choose to use professional development time to review a documentary film or an episode from a content-related field. The primary aim of this form of professional development would be to give teachers access to the information presented. In the same way that a teacher might not bring a specific book or article excerpt into the classroom, teachers may or may not think it is necessary to actually show the film or episode in class in order to bring the information to students. However, teachers who are watching the documentary should be invited to do so while thinking about how the presented content could be applicable to their classroom.

It may well be that a clip of the documentary or a portion of an episode fits in well with the topic that a teacher is instructing. However, it is not necessary. If a documentary were to provide, for example, a biographical insight into F. Scott Fitzgerald's writing inspirations, then the teacher may use that information to make a discussion or lecture more interesting for students, even if the clip itself was not played in class.

DESIGN 4: PROFESSOR COLLABORATION

Researchers have shown that secondary teachers benefit from collaboration with college and university professors, as long as the relationship is collegial and the secondary teachers are treated as partners. Professors are expected to be experts in their field, and a large-scale study completed on the question of "what do the best college teachers do?" found that the one common denominator among excellent professors was their content area mastery. Professors from local colleges and universities could be invited to come and have a conversation with secondary teachers on specific content areas. Secondary teachers may benefit from contact with professors who are masters in certain aspects of content.

Such a form of development must be carefully structured. Secondary teachers should not be "lectured to," but rather invited to engage collegially with individuals who are involved in the creation of new scholarship. Professors might come in with journal articles or project studies to share. They may want to analyze documents together, or simply have a discussion over content area issues that secondary teachers may have had little contact with.

As is the case with the other professional development options, the guiding question for both the professors and the teachers should always be "how can this content be implemented into the classroom?" This does not mean that philosophical or metaphysical questions cannot be explored, since such concepts can be introduced to the classroom, but keeping the level of discussion focused on practical application prevents conversations from getting bogged down in minutia or from becoming too esoteric.

DESIGN 5: TEACHER-LED LESSONS

In many traditional forms of professional development, staff-led professional development activities are the norm. Teachers frequently participate on professional development committees and coordinate activities for a variety of professional development topics. A teacher or group of teachers who are particularly excited about or have a specific expertise in regards to a specific topic of scholarship could be invited to present or teach their content to colleagues.

Teaching lessons to adults, however, is not the same as teaching to students. Adults can engage with the material at a different level, and teacher leaders who volunteer to educate their colleagues should do so with the understanding of the purpose of content area study. A teacher-led lesson should not be a demonstration of the type of lesson that the teacher would give if the audience was made up of secondary students. Rather, the lesson should be designed for an audience of teachers who are all engaged in answering a similar inquiry. The professional development teacher should design the professional development program with the intent of teaching content to her intended audience: her colleagues. Once the information is presented and digested, then a dialogue about how to make that information applicable to the classroom can begin.

KEY POINTS

- The design options discussed in this chapter should be viewed only as possibilities created using scholarly research as a guide. These are merely suggestions as to how content area professional development might be practically applied to schools. Each school has its own unique set of needs and personalities, and a professional development option will likely be most effective if teachers have the ability to shape their own activities so as to address their own needs.
- Even when professional development time is limited—as it often is—teachers who engage in this type of professional development can, over the course of years, build up a considerable amount of content area knowledge even if they engage in no other forms of content area study.
- Researchers looking into what makes teachers effective have pinpointed the level of content area mastery as being a key predictor of teacher effectiveness. In history, for example, a strong content area background is necessary if teachers are to plot a course of historiography through the content.
- If content area learning is such an important part of the recipe for making teachers effective, then it logically follows that ongoing professional development activities should include a content area study component. In Finland, where schools in 2011 were ranked the best in the world by *Newsweek*, teachers are expected to master both content and methods.
- Teachers rarely control what philosophy of professional development their school districts adopt. However, teachers can study content on their own, with the understanding that, by enriching their own content area knowledge, they are enhancing their classroom practice and thus the achievement levels of students. Researchers

indicate that one of the most important things an effective teacher can do is study her content.

- Content area professional development can potentially take many forms, none of which need consume much time. Teachers who study content with the intent of finding ways to work that new knowledge into their classroom become practitioners under the idea of teaching as a field.

THREE

Educating Consilience

Those sciences which are remote from each other cannot be extended without bringing them nearer and forming points of contact between them. —Marquis de Condorcet, 1794

This search and study of the history of the mind, ought not to be confined to one art only. It is by the analogy that one art bears to another, that many things are ascertained, which either were but faintly seen, or, perhaps, would not have been discovered at all, if the inventor had not received the first hints from the practices of a sister art on a similar occasion. The frequent allusion which every man who treats of any art is obliged to make to others, in order to illustrate and confirm his principles, sufficiently show their near connection. . . . —Joshua Reynolds, 1776

The poet or philosopher illustrates his age and country by the efforts of a single mind; but these superior powers of reason or fancy are rare and spontaneous productions. . . . —Edward Gibbon, 1780

Research, synthesis, and practice are entwined in a symbiotic intellectual process. The act of research pushes the boundaries of a field as researchers hunt for evidence that can provide new insights. The process of synthesis combines the research evidence into a new whole. The implementation of these new insights involves practice, which hopefully produces a positive impact.

Secondary teachers rarely if ever engage in research. Science teachers, for example, simply lack the equipment, funding, and possibly the knowledge for delving into that type of activity. History teachers wishing to rifle through evidence to write research reports or books on a topic often find themselves doing so solely in their spare time, with little or no support from the academic institution (likely a high school) where they work.

The public and the academic establishments, because of the history of the university system, often reserve the status of "intellectual" for researchers. High school teachers never appear on the History Channel, and high school science teachers are never invited to speak on *Nova*.

Yet, teaching does involve—or should involve—the act of synthesis and practice. Teachers who double as autodidacts and polymaths, studying widely in search of concepts and insights that can be transferred into the classroom, engage in a process of intense thinking. Discovering ways to implement these insights into the classroom provides a further intellectual challenge. Overcoming such challenges with creativity and perseverance represents the act of teaching and defines teaching as a field.

Medicine provides an analogy that can further an understanding of the point being made here. Research unveils more about the human body, illnesses, or cancers. Doctors synthesize these findings and try to use their greater understanding to logically and scientifically state the case for new treatments. Those new treatments are tested through clinical trials, and the results of those trials inform the daily practice of doctors.

Teachers, similarly, rely on the research of academics, which provides the raw material for synthesis. Once teachers have made the connections themselves and seen the concepts in the material, then a lesson plan is created and implemented (the classroom as clinical trial), and the effectiveness or ineffectiveness of the lesson shapes daily practice.

What follows in this chapter is an argument for an intellectual process called *consilience*. Truly critical thinking includes a cross-curricular component, and good thinkers are always on the lookout for insights in one discipline that might provide a breakthrough in another. Teachers should engage in this kind of thinking and should encourage their students to do so as well.

In the past, dramatic breakthroughs and stunning artistic accomplishments have occurred as a result of chance. Individuals who are capable of making intellectual connections must meet two essential criteria:

1. The individual must live where the "intellectual geography" is conducive to breakthroughs. In the same way that mountain climbers will only exist where there are mountains, scientific geniuses can only exist where the intellectual geography is right. This explains why scientific leaps so often occur in the same place about the same time, such as when Charles Darwin and Alfred Russell Wallace developed evolutionary theory and Gottfried Liebniz and Isaac Newton developed calculus.

2. The individual must be able to concentrate for thousands of hours on end and possess some unique background that allows him or her to make an imaginative leap over intellectual obstacles that have stopped others. Genius cannot be taught, but the personal

> backgrounds of geniuses can be studied and their techniques formalized so as to make the emergence of genius more common.

Historically, such individuals who meet these criteria have been products of accident. Writers, philosophers, and mathematicians are often stereotyped as individuals with less than stellar social skills (some, like Newton, were outright misanthropes). The very nature of the endeavor of artistic, philosophical, or scientific accomplishment necessarily eliminates most social butterflies. Popular and well-adjusted people do not typically find the time to put in ten thousand hours of work studying esoteric subjects and developing unique intellectual skills.

Often, an individual has some biographical reason for shying away from people, some quirk or proclivity that places him or her outside of society (quite often—as in the cases of Wittgenstein, Turing, or Da Vinci, and possibly and probably Nietzsche and Newton—the factor was once-frowned-upon homosexuality), makes him or her uncomfortable with people, and causes him or her to seek comfort in matters of the intellect. Being asocial is not a precondition for genius, but the hard work of intellectual achievement cannot be completed at a cocktail party.

Despite the stereotype of the "mad genius," we need not worry that brilliant insights can only be gathered close to the border of insanity. The correlation between genius and mental illness or social dysfunction can be explained in that few well-adjusted and psychologically secure people find comfort in the cold airs of intellectual or creative frontiers. In fact, the genius–madness correlation is just that—a correlation.

No fine line exists between creative genius and insanity; it is simply that individuals with backgrounds that make them uncomfortable with society often find comfort in intellectual endeavors and then stumble upon patterns in information that no one else has seen before. This process can be demystified and turned into a formal educational philosophy.

Information is now made available in cheaply procured and easily accessed forms. This increases the likelihood that individuals can see novel patterns in the information. Some of the environmental bars to the creation of genius, such as coercive governmental or religious systems that are suspicious of free thought, a limited access to information, or poor mathematical hardware (the Romans suppressed Western mathematics for centuries due to their fondness for the cumbersome Roman numeral system) have been removed in the West. The environment is right for the development of genius; all that remains is to prepare future human minds properly.

Michael Shermer (2011) calls the brain's ability to find constellations in the informational sky "patternicity" and gives good evolutionary reasons for why the brain searches for it. However, as Shermer has also noted, not all patterns are valid. In fact, a good many geniuses have embraced a pattern-based type of thinking that leaves them open to embracing conspiracies or logical fallacies. Proper pattern-seeking techniques must be taught, lest educators lead their students into illogical thinking.

An educational program that teaches students to think in patterns and to superimpose and adjust patterns learned from one set of facts onto questions posed in another field increases the likelihood of breakthroughs. Formalizing this system into a philosophy of education means that advances in the intellectual fields will no longer have to rely on serendipity.

Not all individuals will push scientific frontiers, but the search for patterns and the application of learned connections across disciplines is called, by another name, *thinking*, and schools should be deeply invested in the creation of people who can do it. A potential criticism of this system is that it leaves little room for the group-based education so currently in vogue.

Yet, groups of ill-informed individuals are of little use in problem-solving, and even skills used in a team setting must be acquired individually. Individuals with "downloaded" patterns from various backgrounds can share information and insights, but again, individual brains must be individually educated before they are of much use in such a group endeavor.

An argument for such an approach to education has roots in a concept known as consilience. The term is defined as the process that occurs when "an Induction, obtained from one class of facts, coincides with an Induction obtained from another different class" (as quoted in Snyder 2011, p. 332) and was coined by the 19th-century Cambridge don William Whewell.

Edward O. Wilson (1998) further shaped the term, describing consilience as a way to link concepts across disciplines. Practically speaking, and to paraphrase Wilson, there are two types of thinkers. There are those who research in a single field, pushing the boundaries in search of the all-important scientific discovery, and then there are those who combine discoveries and make connections across disciplines.

The second type of thinker sees that certain truths that can be induced from one set of facts (say, mathematical) can also be induced from studying a different set of facts (say, historical). Evolutionary biology, for example, has a high level of consilience because the principle of evolution can be induced by studying fossils, genetic evidence, or even technological change. Secondary education must embrace consilience, since the act of connecting and unifying facts across disciplines to solve problems is central to critical thinking.

At the secondary level, we seek not to create researchers, but critical thinkers who can study and manipulate facts for a purpose. This thinking ability is what allows for further intellectual discovery. It counters the false notion that the emphasis in secondary schools should be tilted heavily toward math and science.

Although, clearly, math and science are important, it is not historically true that great scientific or mathematical leaps follow from immersing students in those subjects. In fact, the greatest scientific and intellectual breakthroughs in history have come from individuals who have approached mathematical and scientific problems with a fresh perspective, one often gained from having a history of thinking in another discipline.

The noted philosopher of science Thomas Kuhn observed: "Almost always the men who achieve these fundamental inventions of a new paradigm have been either very young or very new to the field whose paradigm they change" (1996, p. 90). Scientists or thinkers of a certain generation tend to have their thinking on certain questions calcified; only when someone comes in with a fresh perspective or novel background to look at a problem are breakthroughs made.

Examples of this in the history of science are abundant. Newton made his leaps by ignoring the stagnant Cambridge curriculum; instead, he began with big questions about the universe and started with first principles to answer them. Faraday was an interested amateur with a gift for devising experiments. Einstein thought of novel questions, then approached the process of answering them from first principles, almost totally ignoring the scientific and mathematical establishment in his quest. Jared Diamond approached history from the perspective of a biologist and, beginning with principles of evolution, set out to answer some of history's biggest questions.

August Kekulé, a pioneer in organic chemistry, originally was trained in architecture before entering chemistry, and Peter Watson noted that Kekulé "Later . . . argued that his architectural training (such as it was) had helped him to think in pictures—and this played a vital role when he came to identify the structure of carbon compounds" (2010, p. 278). Likewise, Masha Gessen wrote that the modern genius Grigory Perelman proved the Poincaré Conjecture by "applying Alexandrov spaces to Geometrization" (2009, p. 122) and uniting various concepts from different mathematical backgrounds.

Clearly, not every student will reach the level of these individuals. However, piano teachers still instruct their students to play the works of Beethoven. Anyone looking to gain a workable talent in the playing of the piano does well to mimic the patterns of the masters. Society does need geniuses, and proper training at the secondary level will no doubt facilitate the creation of geniuses, but critical thinking skills are important for any endeavor. And, as any scholar or reader will tell you, the ability to think in such a way is pleasurable for its own sake.

New findings in neuroscience indicate that the brain's pattern-seeking capabilities are what make it a unique instrument for thinking in the animal kingdom. The argument for adding consilience as a core concept of education can be made from a different approach as well, not just historically, as noted above, but from brain science.

KEY POINTS

- The "environment" for the creation of genius is now well-formed in the West as no governmental or religious organizations can formally punish free thinking, and information is thoroughly democratized.
- In the past, "geniuses" have been seen as individuals with asocial tendencies or as people on the border of sanity. This has led to a mystification of the genius. Yet, these asocial tendencies are merely a correlation as great thinkers must necessarily spend thousands of hours in solitude developing their skills, and few socially well-adjusted people will do so.
- Great thinkers typically develop patterns of thought from studying one set of facts, then superimposing those patterns onto problems from a different field, and this has frequently led to scientific paradigm shifts in the past and great intellectual breakthroughs.
- The concept of thinking in a cross-curricular way, searching for patterns in one set of facts that can be later synthesized and applied through novel application to problems in another field, is called *consilience*. To teach consilience is to teach students to think. Not everyone will be a historically defined genius, but everyone can learn to think.

FOUR

Neuroscience and Consilience

Facts, whether narrow or extensive, and conclusions suggested by them, whether many or few, do not constitute, even when combined, reflective thought. The suggestions must be organized; they must be arranged with reference to one another and with reference to the facts on which they depend for proof. When the factors of facility, of fertility, and of depth are properly balance or proportioned, we get as the outcome continuity of thought. —John Dewey, 1910

Brain research rarely creates new philosophies, but it does vindicate some old ones. —David Brooks

No gimmicks. If you want to get a lot out of reading, read a lot; if you want to get better at remembering errands or birthdays, practice remembering errands or birthdays. No shortcuts, no cross-training —*no Sudoku.* —Steven Pinker

Few words are more intimidating than "neuroscience." This word, conjuring up as it does images of embarrassingly complicated dendrites, synapses, and neuronal pathways would seem to represent something so complex that its integration into education is impossible.

At one level, this is true. Anybody who hopes to study the goop of the brain and derive any kind of practical educational philosophy from it will no doubt face disappointment. On another level, however, neuroscience can provide important insights into how people learn. As of yet, neuroscience has not had the effect of overturning the field of education and the development of methods. In fact, findings from brain research, as will be argued in the meat of the forthcoming chapter, tend to provide scientific backing to long-established forms of best practice in education.

It may come to be that neuroscience will not overturn educational practice but rather will be altered itself by its convergence with education. The effects of early education on the development of neuronal path-

27

ways in the brain, for example, most likely will serve to give scientific credence to what educators and parents consider obvious.

Much of what we now know about the brain is in alignment with previous educational practice. The technology necessary to study the brain in action evolved only recently, so neuroscience remains a relatively new discipline. Educators looking to implement neuroscientific findings into the classroom or educational theorists looking to integrate those findings into a philosophy should necessarily proceed with caution. However, the implications of findings in neuroscience can be so important for the field of teaching that we should definitely proceed.

At any rate, teachers should view the science of understanding the brain as a partner in daily classroom practice, even if we do have to rely on secondary sources, in the form of neuroscientists, to tell us what is happening in the very complex machinery of the brain.

Imagine going back in time some two hundred thousand years, adopting a baby from a hunter-gatherer tribe on the African savannah, and bringing that child into modern civilization. The process of educating that baby to understand the world around her would require an enormous outpouring of resources and effort.

This is not a science fiction scenario, but the everyday work of parenting and education. The DNA of a human being is, on average, virtually identical to the DNA of our hunter-gatherer ancestors. Civilization has grown around us, largely through a process of cultural synthesis and technological evolution (explained in the connect-the-dots examples in a later chapter). Yet, newborn children are, genetically, almost unchanged since humanity's early migratory years on the savannah.

The human mind, then, is not "wired" for civilization. The acts of reading, writing, working through complex mathematics, and understanding abstract economic or philosophical concepts are examples of what the human mind can do with training, not what it originally evolved to do.

So difficult is the process of remolding the brain that some psychologists now speak of a "10,000-hour rule," in which 10,000 hours of practice are virtually required to wire the body and mind so that they are expert at performing surgery or a virtuoso piece on the piano, for example.

Think of a ballerina or gymnast using her body to complete intricate (and seemingly painful) moves. The legs, back, and abdomen did not evolve for the purpose of flipping through the air, but with dedicated training such moves can be completed and the muscles remolded. Martial arts experts can use their hands and legs to complete moves well beyond the purposes of grasping and walking for which they originally evolved.

Any high school teacher is familiar with the duality of human nature, between our naturally evolved instincts and the higher-level thought of which the mind is capable. Certain periods of the day—lunch and passing periods—bring out the latent nature of adolescents. No one has to teach teenagers how to flirt, jockey for position and seek security within a group, or challenge authority. Their DNA has been doing this for millions of years (even in pre-human form). After school, students like nothing better than to gather into groups and make simulated warfare of some kind or other (usually involving a form of ball) against "tribes" from other schools.

The work of the classroom, which so many kids find so difficult, involves the education of that hunter-gatherer mind, the remolding of it into something capable of working with abstract concepts. This difficult work can be assisted with insights from the field of neuroscience.

As early as 2001, researchers into the field of neuroscience were noting that the field was mature enough to warrant integration into classroom practice. A growing number of researchers are indicating that teacher training should take place with theories of cognition in mind, with some even stating that teachers are responsible for shaping students' brains.

Neuroscientific implications for the classroom are not particularly startling. One researcher, Herbert Simon, stated that "The connection between cognition and instruction lies, of course, in learning . . . " (2001, p. 205). Simon then noted that incorporating findings from neuroscience into the classroom is not as daunting as it might appear since many educational theories and techniques are already in alignment with what brain research indicates. He stated that many cognitive theories "might even be mistaken for common sense" (p. 211).

Longstanding educational practice is largely in alignment with the findings of neuroscience. Time and again, modern scientific suggestions for classroom practice fall into alignment with age-old educational practice. Going back to 1910, John Dewey published a book called *How We Think*, in which he called for problem-centered classrooms designed around the way in which young people interact with facts, beginning with their experiences—advice that mirrors modern findings in neuroscience. In 1938, well before neuroscience came of age, John Dewey called for learner-centered activities in which teachers and students are involved in interacting with their environment.

What neuroscience does indicate is that cross-curricular thinking can create associations in the mind, between one field to the next. Studies of the brain have revealed that after the brain receives sensory information from the eyes and ears, these are transferred into electrical impulses and turned into higher level cognition by the temporal lobes. In 1949, scientists noted that neurons activated in tandem tended to fire simultaneously again in the future. (Anecdotal evidence bears this out—think of how songs or movies can trigger memories uniquely related in your past history.)

More modern researchers suggest that neurons, when they fire at the same time, become wired together. Patricia Wolfe (2001) notes the educational implications of such a finding and explains that teachers should try to stimulate various sensory organs while instructing, so that students solidify neurological patterns. Drawing connections and seeing patterns in the classroom cause neurological restructuring in the brain.

This is a bit of a digression, but psychiatry may have co-opted the idea of connections and patterns forming under the cognitive surface. Beginning with Herbart in 1824, and later popularized by Freud, was the concept that ideas often connect unconsciously to form patterns in the subconscious. Modern research would more likely indicate that these patterns are formed beneath the surface, in a kind of "muscle memory" for the brain. At any rate, the concept of underlying patterns may be more useful if detached from the mysticism that influenced much of the early development of psychology.

To use another example of how nothing is really new under the microscope: In 1886, James Cattell suggested that this underlying pattern of connections allows for flash decision-making, a point recently rediscovered by Malcolm Gladwell in 2005. Furthermore, language specialists point to a language instinct in the brain, a relic of the fact that spoken language developed well before written language. Children, for example, learn to talk with no formal training at all, but cannot learn to write simply by soaking it up from their environment in the same way.

To touch on an earlier point, at birth, the human brain has essentially the same physical makeup that it had prior to the development of civilization. Separate parts of the brain evolved for different purposes and at different points in human evolution, something that can lead to internal conflict between deep-seated urges and what the intellect understands to be appropriate.

Perhaps this notion, too, has its antecedents in the world of thought. The great theologian St. Augustine most eloquently described the split nature of humanity in his work "The Two Cities," in which he showed how human urges came into conflict with what he believed to be the more spiritual side of human nature. Strip the theology away from his writings and they make for a pretty good biological treatise on the human brain. Development of the intellect thus often involves educating the subconscious brain and taking into accounting the conflicting nature of consciousness.

The fields of education, cognitive neuroscience, and educational psychology synthesized into a field called mind, brain, and education (MBE) science, which was a concept derived almost simultaneously in disparate parts of the world between 2002 and 2009. As a discipline, MBE seeks to unite different fields and integrate new ideas.

As a new field, it remains beset by a series of logical tangles and, occasionally, falls prey to the trendy (i.e., the notion that teachers should refer to themselves as "mind, brain, education scientists"), but none of this disqualifies the merits of the field. Still in its infancy, MBE is best described as a perspective on teaching and knowledge, one that calls for teachers and scientists to share information across disciplines for the purpose of making connections.

How does all of this inform daily practice for the teacher? Findings in neuroscience can be distilled into a few practical maxims for classroom guidance.

1. Facts are to thinking what stars are to constellations or dots are to connect-the-dots games. Daniel Willingham (2009), a neuroscientist who specializes in applying brain studies to education, has noted the importance of facts as a basis for making connections. One has to have something to think about before one can think. And when the brain receives stimuli in tandem, those stimuli tend to be wired closely together in the brain.

2. The brain has the potential to think abstractly, but reading, writing, and thinking mathematically do not come naturally to a brain that evolved for separate purposes. The brain does naturally look for patterns in information, but this must be formalized and perfected lest the thinker fall prey to seeing illogical patterns.

3. Education should be viewed as the training of thought process skills. Students cannot learn to play the violin by watching the teacher play, filling out a worksheet on the basics of the violin, and then taking a state-mandated exam. Students might pass exams under this system but be completely ignorant of how to actually play a violin. Real education involves helping students to practice thinking skills by manipulating information. To really educate someone in the skills of reading comprehension, writing, and abstract thinking to a high level will likely take thousands of hours of immersion.

The interior of the field of neuroscience remains intimidating even to expert practitioners, so extrapolating from rather arcane facts should not be attempted by dilettantes. However, a good many neuroscientists have made their research findings accessible to the secondary practitioner who may find that information useful for educational practice, and this chapter is built upon that secondary work. Teachers and researchers should not fear that neuroscientific findings will overturn long-established forms of best practice, but rather should view neuroscience as a partner in the development of classroom activities.

However, if the process of education is understood to be the "civilization" of the mind, then certain concepts of what the brain does and how it evolved can be useful for classroom application. The brain wires together concepts when facts are connected and reinforced. This process develops patterns of thought and alters the stuff of the mind on a neurological level.

Admittedly, this chapter presents a rather clean and somewhat abstract view of neuroscience and education. Teachers reading it may be skeptical of its practical applications when trying to educate groups of students who may not have read the most recent research by Steven Pinker and therefore not get the purpose of the exercise.

In his book, *The Social Animal: The Hidden Sources of Love, Character, and Achievement*, David Brooks (2012) admirably captured the act of teaching:

> Ms. Taylor would look out over a sea of faces in her classes. She'd have to remind herself that those flaccid and bored expressions are deceiving. There's mayhem within. When she puts a piece of information in front of a student, that kid's brain doesn't just absorb it in some easily understandable fashion. As John Medina writes, the process is more "like a blender left running with the lid off. The information is literally sliced into discrete pieces as it enters the brain and splattered all over the insides of our mind." "Don't exaggerate the orderliness of their thoughts," she'd tell herself. The best she could hope to do was to merge old patterns already there with new patterns from what she was trying to teach. (p. 81)

Quite right. Teaching is hard, students often recalcitrant, and the environment teachers must work within often nearly impossible. This chapter and this book offer only arguments for doing the best that can be done, and neuroscience provides an important tool for achieving that aim.

KEY POINTS

- Civilization is relatively new to human culture, and humans have the same hunter-gatherer DNA that they possessed 100,000 years ago. Reading, writing, mathematics, and abstract thinking are examples of what the brain can do with intense training, but these things do not come naturally to the mind any more than elaborate gymnastics techniques come naturally to the back and legs.
- Findings in neuroscience have not overturned good educational theory and practice, but rather have mostly substantiated what has long been known by expert practitioners and theorists. The field is made less intimidating for educators if we focus on the secondary literature, in which neuroscientists distill their findings into practical advice.
- Facts are to thinking what stars are to constellations or dots are to a connect-the-dots game. Facts must be manipulated if thinkers are to see novel patterns in the information and think critically. Arguments are buttressed by facts, and thinking is progressed often by the discovery of new facts.

- The mind does naturally seek patterns and tends to wire facts together with stimuli as they are learned. Education should be viewed as the development of abstract thinking skills in students, similar to teaching someone to play the violin, and it must be understood that such skills can only be learned by intensive immersion in the work of reading, writing, and thinking.

FIVE

Applications for Principals and Education Professors

The media often portrays the principal as a demanding person who takes charge and directs everyone to accomplish results. These leaders use fear to control their subordinates. This popular concept of the principal as a strong-fisted person is giving way to a new type of leadership. Many school leaders discarded that model of leadership decades ago and now share with others in making decisions for improved teaching and learning. — Marilyn Katzenmeyer and Gayle Moller, 2001

In sports we have developed a culture in which, based on intuitive feelings of correlation, a team's success or failure is often attributed largely to the ability of the coach. As a result, when teams fail, the coach is often fired. Mathematical analysis of firings in all major sports, however, has shown that those firings had, on average, no effect on team performance. — Leonard Mlodinow, 2008

Teachers are the primary audience for this book, because teachers are the individuals who can most easily facilitate a philosophical change. As stated earlier, any educational method that depends on large-scale structural reforms risks getting tied up in politics or delayed by bureaucracy. Teachers need not wait for changes in professional development activities, school structure, or state and federal law to implement a changing concept of the profession. This being said, should principals or professors of education choose to embrace the philosophy of teaching as a field espoused here, that philosophy could guide structural changes in teacher training and teacher professional development.

What is proposed in this chapter is a larger scale theory for how teacher training at the collegiate level and the role of the principal would change if the concept of teaching as a field were to be embraced. Typically speaking, large-scale political reform for education involves creating a

35

structure of rewards or punishments designed to create change from the top down. In the new scheme, the role of the principal is to create conditions that would foster change from the bottom up.

For education professors, embracing the philosophy espoused here would entail a new form of educational training. The current model of university training for potential teachers separates the instruction of content and methods. Students learn content from Ph.D.s (or graduate students) in certain disciplines. Students learn methods from their professors of education, but the two spheres rarely, if ever, connect.

The notion, then, is that students will learn content and methods separately but apply one to the other at some point in practice. This process could be streamlined and made more effective if education professors trained students in ways to directly process specific forms of content into classroom application, thereby training teachers how to engage in the work that is their field.

Students of biology, for example, engage in the same type of work that biologists do in practice. The field of education, defined as the process of applying methods to content for the classroom application, would provide a context for university courses in education. Students who learned how to study widely, see patterns and connections, then apply methods for the classroom while university students would likely take this notion with them into their careers as teachers.

PRINCIPALS

Much research into the concepts of teacher leadership and professional learning communities cites the importance of nonhierarchical school structures. Such an approach is an analogous to the way doctors are treated in a hospital or professors in a university, and calls for increased roles for teachers. Traditional school structures, however, maintain a top-down design, in which authority is invested in the principal and the administrative team.

Shirley M. Hord (2004) and others have researched the impact of professional learning communities (PLCs) on school environments. Hord, who worked with the Southwest Educational Development Laboratory, studied a school in that organization's region that was noted for its successes. She wrote of the atmosphere there:

> The school staff saw themselves as a community of learners where the entire school learned together—teachers, parents, and students. They all shared a common vision of what the school should accomplish and what type of environment it should have. Teachers were innovative and encouraged to reflect on their practice. They were involved in shared decision making. If conflict occurred it was shared openly and resolved. (p. 1)

Although a thorough discussion of school communities and the role of PLCs is beyond the scope of this book, it is worth noting that a slew of new educational researchers are calling for the tearing down of school hierarchies. In highly effective schools, teachers take ownership of the vision and involve themselves in activities and decisions beyond the classroom.

Somewhat ironically, because of the traditionalist (indeed feudal) nature of most schools, the principal is the only person with the authority to deconstruct these hierarchies. Hord wrote, "Shared leadership emerged as a critical component of successful professional learning communities—and yet, the level of shared leadership achieved, turned out to be almost entirely dependent upon the principal's willingness to share authority and his or her ability to motivate teachers to take on new responsibilities" (p. 2).

As has been repeatedly stated, teachers in any type of school, regardless of leadership, can embrace the philosophy laid out in these pages. However, a principal who embraces such a philosophy and wants to move her staff toward viewing teaching as a field under the principles described here would have to share leadership and redefine her role. The major role of a principal who embraced the idea of teaching as a field would be to encourage this shifting concept of teaching in the teachers in her school.

Thus, the principal would be responsible for deconstructing hierarchies and encouraging teacher contemplation and study through professional development activities. Also, principals can enforce accountability be rewarding teacher products with positive evaluations, or even by producing school-wide journals to celebrate teacher lessons.

In application, this would mean that, instead of paying for outside speakers to deliver professional development seminars to teachers, time would be given over to the study of content. Principals would encourage teachers to understand that their level of content area mastery is a key piece of teacher effectiveness. To use an earlier example, a good school climate acts like a greenhouse, creating the right conditions under which ideas can grow. Principals are the individuals responsible for constructing this greenhouse, but to do so they must first embrace a changing concept of their job.

EDUCATION PROFESSORS

Currently, education remains a field unto itself, one separate from the secondary classroom. Education as a field involves the development of methods training in future teachers. Much of this methods training is guided by educational researchers who conduct studies that inquire into the effectiveness or noneffectiveness of practices in schools. This is all necessary and important work. The emphasis placed on content area study in this book is not intended to denigrate expertise in methods, but to provide balance.

Research into teacher effectiveness has indicated, time and again, the importance of teacher content area knowledge. If education is a scientific field, then it must alter conceptions based upon the evidence. Obviously, one vital role of public schools is to provide a place that exemplifies the American values of multiculturalism and to provide all citizens with a basic educational background that allows them to participate in a demo-cratic republic.

But we should never lose sight of the fact that the primary job of a school is to teach students how to think. As a teacher, my role requires me to teach students content and skills, and this endeavor consumes the bulk of my time. To define the essential mission of public schools in any other way severely interferes with the seriousness of education.

Ruby Payne's book *A Framework for Understanding Poverty* represented the nadir of this wing of social education. In her strikingly frivolous work, Payne compiled a series of vagaries (example: "the typical pattern in poverty for discipline is to verbally chastise the child, or physically beat the child, then forgive and feed him/her" (1996, p. 23) backed by absolutely no evidence. Based upon these stereotypes, Payne built a rope ladder to the moon. She appeared to argue that the central mission of school was to educate impoverished students in the "hidden rules" of the middle class.

No, it is not. Schools exist to teach students academic skills. Worries about shifting the mission of schools away from the study of content go back to the *Nation at Risk* findings from 1983, which Diane Ravitch (2010) characterized as "the steady erosion of the content of the curriculum" (pp. 24–25). In one study, conducted by Oser and Baeriswyl in 2001, the authors warned of what can happen if content in the classroom is de-emphasized, something the authors called "therapy-i-zation," which got in the way of learning:

> Instead of taking both the process activity and the interaction dynamic into account, only social cohesion or experiences of autonomy and sim-ilar dynamic variables are considered. These conditions are important, of course, to consider, but they must be connected to the learning of content. In one of our interviews, a boy said, "You know, our teacher is so good-hearted, and we love each other so much, but we do not learn anything." (2001, p. 1033)

These are not fringe notions in the field of education, where scholars can still be taken seriously even while writing sentences such as this: "The educational answer to the angst of early adolescence is mainly to be found not in more curriculum but in stronger community" (Hargreaves, p. 61).

We must remember that a third of teachers leave the profession within the first three years, and it is possible that the public perception of teaching as a lowly paid version of charity work, or that teachers care about but kids don't really know much content, affects such a high turnover. One teacher who left the profession stated that she quit because she felt that "society does not consider teaching to be serious intellectual work" (Clayton & Schoonmaker, 2003, p. 253). This is but one comment, but this teacher speaks for many others. It is impossible to imagine that medicine or law loses many students for similar reasons.

This focus on educational factors that fall outside the realm of curriculum, content, and learning is but one problem with education as a field. The other issue involves the emphasis of scholars on the wildly impractical. It has been popular, in recent years, for scholars to write articles that read as policy recommendations. Since few politicians read educational journals, and since there is little of value for practical application in these arguments for teachers, the purpose of these articles is unclear.

Studies in education serve a purpose only if they explain to educators what lessons can be taken from the study of other school systems and be immediately applied in the classroom. Educational research that lacks a focus on direct implementation is of no use to anyone. Educators cannot control external factors in politics or society; we can only control the day-to-day activities of our classroom, and the focus of education should be to enhance that practice.

The message to professors of education is this: Invite future teachers to engage in and shape a field of practice. Teach them the tools necessary to use methods specific to certain forms of content, and then explain that this intellectually serious process should continue on throughout their entire teaching careers.

SIX

Applications for Various Academic Disciplines

Even the hardest of hard sciences is replete with assumptions that may be fairly classified as metaphysical. Almost all mathematicians, for example, presume that they are discovering, rather than creating, mathematical truths. Ask a roomful of mathematicians whether three was a prime number a billion years ago (ie: before there were humans to define it as such) and every hand will go up. And yet to say so is to espouse the metaphysical position that primeness and all the other subject matter of mathematics have a reality independent of the human mind. This assumption goes under various names, one of which is Mathematical Platonism. —Neal Stephenson, 2003

We are living in the middle of a revolution in consciousness. Over the past few years, geneticists, neuroscientists, psychologists, sociologists, economists, anthropologists, and others have made great strides in understanding the building blocks of human flourishing. And a core finding of their works is that we are not primarily the products of conscious thinking. We are primarily the products of thinking that happens below the level of awareness. —David Brooks, 2012

Our brains are just not wired to do probability problems very well. —Richard Feynman

Extraordinary claims require extraordinary evidence. —Carl Sagan

In this final chapter before moving into Part II, which includes examples of practical classroom activities created using the philosophy presented here, it is worthwhile to address potential applications for the methodology in various academic areas. Part II has practical examples from the discipline of world history, but the principles of education that guided their creation can be adapted to other fields.

Teachers of mathematics, science, or grammar may balk at the notion of introducing the classroom philosophy stated here, thinking that grammar and mathematics work by memorization and the application of structured rules.

Yet, those who study evolutionary biology can see Darwinian connections in living things or forms of technology. Those who are fluent in French can translate English in their mind and create thoughts in languages that have various levels of expressions. Students of linguistics can generally dissect a word into its historic origins and see human language as an expression of several thousand years of evolution.

Perhaps the goal of education in subjects such as mathematics and the sciences should be altered. Instead of training students how to complete Mendelian charts and "plug and chug" through formulas, it would be more effective to train students to have a mathematical or scientific mindset.

Teachers of foreign languages often immerse students, forcing them to listen and understand new words and forms of syntax until a state of comprehension known as *fluency* is achieved. To be fluent means to be able to make sense of the world in the light of a new language and to communicate in the terms of this language. The goal of teachers of mathematics and the sciences should also be to make students fluent in their understanding and to see the world through the prism of mathematics or the scientific method.

Social studies teachers and enthusiasts grind their teeth to nubs every time some smart-alecky journalist points to the results of some survey on the topic of historical literacy. The results of these pop quizzes are often embarrassing, to be sure, and are always the cause of a good deal of hand-wringing among those who care about such minor issues as the continuation of the American Republic. This being said, historical illiteracy is but one of many such illiteracies that can be uncovered with a survey.

Of all the errors and fallacies that pox public discourse, a misunderstanding of odds and probabilities is perhaps the greatest, which is a shame, since the inability to understand mathematics and probabilities can have serious repercussions.

There is a good reason for bringing this up. Teachers of mathematics often struggle with the concept of making mathematics relevant for students. Yet, imagine how excited a department of math teachers might be after reading an essay from Ian Stewart (2010) called "Behind the Scenes: The Hidden Mathematics That Rules Our World," which appears as a chapter in a book on the history of the first scientific organization in the world, London's Royal Society.

Stewart begins:

The role of most sciences is relatively obvious, but mathematics is far less visible than engineering or biology. However, this lack of visibility does not imply that mathematics has no useful applications. On the contrary, mathematics underpins much of today's technology, and is vital to virtually all areas of human activity. (p. 342)

The same concept, beginning with Stewart's assertion, can be applied to mathematics. Stewart laments that "you don't have to know any mathematics, or even be aware of its existence, to use the technology that it enables" (p. 346). Yet, beginning from a perspective of a modern technology, then unraveling the mathematics behind its function might be an effective way to teach mathematics and to alter the way that students react to their environment.

Stewart gives a lesson on how Newtonian mathematics was applied to every aspect of NASA's rover landing on the moon, but also notes that "Next time you listen to a CD while driving along the motorway in your car, and hit a bump, you may care to ask yourself why the CD player skips tracks only if it's a really big bump—big enough to risk damaging your wheel" (p. 349).

Wouldn't this be an interesting way to begin a lesson? Sort of like asking students why the sound of a jet always seems to come from far behind the plane. One level of explanation is that the jet can move faster than the sound it produces, and the engine noise follows the plane like a skier being dragged by rope. This explanation, while not wrong, is not as descriptive as another explanation, which is that light from the plane reaches your eyes faster than the sound waves do. This causes someone on the ground to experience the plane and engine noise differently than someone actually in the jet would. Understanding the discrepancy in the way observers perceive natural phenomena paves the way for students to understand Einstein's Theory of Relativity.

After posing this question, Stewart describes a "history of answer," which involves a strange mid 19th-century sort of algebra developed by George Boole, a British professor at Queen's College. Stewart describes the logic:

> [Boole's] most significant work was his 1854 book *An Investigation of the Laws of Thought*. In it, he reformulated logic in terms of algebra—but a very strange kind of algebra. Most of the familiar algebraic rules, such as $x + y = y + x$, are valid in Boole's logical realm, but there are some surprises, such as $1 + 1 = 0$. Here 1 means "true," 0 means "false," and $x + y$ means what computer scientists now call "exclusive or'" either x is true or y is true, *but not both*. The first formula says that this statement does not depend on the order in which the two statements x and y are considered. The second says that if x and y are both true, then $x + y$ is false—because the definition of + includes the requirement "not both." (p. 350)

Stewart claims that Boolean algebra, like Liebniz's binary code, was not considered practically applicable until the Computer Age began, the notion being that algebra did not have to be written in numbers, but could be the creation of any "mathematical concepts or structures that can be manipulated symbolically according to a fixed system of rules" (p. 351). When the great medieval Muslim thinker Al-Khwarizmi created *al-jabr* (algebra), he worked only through a single symbolic construct. It is possible to create different algebraic rules for new needs.

Answering practical questions using scientific or mathematical answers not only teaches students how to use mathematical formulas, but opens them up to the broader world of metaphysics. *Metaphysics*, a term created by Aristotle and meaning "beyond physics," involves thinking about how one is thinking. Metaphysical questions get at the bedrock notion of the validity of the process.

The result would be students who are mathematically fluent, in the sense that they could derive mathematical principles from everyday occurrences. Even if they could not always work out the calculations, at least they would be aware of the mathematics underpinning the world around them. Stewart notes that the myriad of doodads now available on the market, from iPods to video games (those soul-sucking machines that lobotomize young men), all have algebraic systems embedded in them.

This awareness, at the very least, would engender some respect for mathematicians. Stewart writes, "If neither the media, nor the public, nor even practicing scientists realize that this hidden mathematics exists, we will strop training mathematicians, and the necessary people will cease to exist too" (p. 352).

Math teachers who read essays such as Stewart's might find themselves armed and energized to reconfigure classroom curriculum. Students who see the practical applications of abstract mathematics, and who view it as a dynamic structure with rules that can be altered depending upon needs, might be more likely to continue studying math than would those who merely see mathematics as a series of exercises that are only worthwhile for attaining scores on tests.

Likewise, immersion in probabilities can have benefits beyond just realizing that buying lotto tickets or rooting for the Cubs is a bad investment. For one thing, understanding probabilities can make bowling more fun. Next time you bowl and knock over one or two pins on the side, jump up and down and shout "Do you know how *unlikely* that was?" Prior to releasing the ball, any configuration of pins had a certain rather high statistical unlikelihood, some more unlikely than the coveted strike.

You can do the same while playing golf or hitting baseballs if you like. Statistically speaking, prior to your baseball bat or golf club swing the odds are long that the ball will end up in any particular place. Therefore, no matter where the ball falls, it lands in a statistically unlikely place.

The reason it's odd to jump up and down after hitting a golf ball into the rough or knocking over one or two pins is that things are only statistically improbable before they occur. This sounds obvious, but misunderstandings about odds and probabilities wreak havoc in lives all of the time.

Once one understands probabilities and randomness, watching the news can become a gut-twisting exercise in frustration. Although the media may enjoy interviewing cancer survivors who stopped treatment and found remission by chanting or through homeopathic healing, the reality is that such interviews do nothing but highlight an effect of randomness known as a *sampling error*.

Hundreds of thousands of people get cancer every year: some will go into "spontaneous" remission (perhaps as a result of the immune system fighting the cancer or as a result of any number of mysterious occurrences at the still poorly understood molecular level of cancer) and will likely claim to have gone into remission as a result of alternative medicine. However, a proper statistical sample would likely show that of all the people who stop the scientifically approved treatment, a good many get worse. No one interviews them.

Such media practices are dangerous in that individuals who see such outlier cases in a media interview may stop a scientifically based treatment and not be so lucky. We all know or know of chain smokers who dodged lung cancer and other tobacco-related diseases, but since we also know or know of many more people who developed horrendous health problems as a result of smoking, one may make an evidence-based decision to avoid lighting up.

To take another example from the sciences, once one has properly studied Evolutionary Theory, the world no longer looks the same. The simple act of looking at a clock suddenly becomes an object in Darwin's master thesis. A clock is but one species in a large evolutionary bush that includes watches, towers, and even digital applications for cell phones.

All modern clocks trace their lineage to a single ancestor called the sundial that evolved to meet the needs of various environments. Saturation in evolutionary theory becomes a mindset, as the same concepts can be applied to other forms of technology (in his book *Connections*, James Burke [2007] includes a fascinating evolutionary history of the television set) and helps to make sense of fears about global change. In the past, shifts in the climate or in society have created new conditions that old diseases suddenly find accommodating.

Teachers who study widely in their fields can easily come across such insights offered by mathematicians and scientists. The goal of a class would be to make students fluent in forms of mathematical or scientific thought. Teachers would have to figure out ways to bring this notion into their own classrooms, but by conceiving of their profession as a field of creative practice, new types of curriculum could be created to develop new types of students.

KEY POINTS

- Teachers of mathematics and the sciences should seek to create students who are fluent in the mindset of those topics. Teachers of mathematics should strive to get students to see underlying mathematical principles in the everyday world.
- Questions of metaphysics can open up an understanding of mathematics as a creative endeavor with rules that can be shifted depending upon needs, rather than as a rigid construct that requires mere memorization of techniques.
- Studies of biology or probabilities can be applied to everyday life, with individuals becoming "fluent" in the understanding of probabilities, something that will likely prove worthwhile when making decisions.

Part II

Connecting the Dots

[A]ll your grand principles, which I understand very well, would do splendidly in books and very badly in practice. In your plans for reform, you are forgetting the difference between our two positions: you work only on paper which accepts anything, is smooth and flexible and offers no obstacles either to your imagination or your pen, while I, poor empress, work on human skin, which is far more sensitive and touchy.
—Catherine II, to the philosopher Denis Diderot, 1774

The arguments put forth in Part I were intended to give historical and scientific backing to the formation of a philosophy that could be easily put into application in classrooms. As Catherine II reminded the great encyclopedist Denis Diderot, theory is worth very little if it cannot be ingested and applied by practitioners. The purpose, then, of Part II is to provide examples of how the lessons from the history and philosophy of science, education, and neuroscience described in Part I can actually be used in the classroom.

Everything begins with the teacher, so lessons of the type described in this section require that teachers be masters of their content. Teachers must take the time to see patterns themselves before students can be trained to see them. There is no other way. If real education is to be achieved, teachers cannot merely act as "facilitators" in an already formed educational system, merely passing out the requisite materials, keeping order in the room, and ensuring that standardized test scores are high.

If real academic achievement is to be made by students, teachers must be seen as dynamic individuals involved in the formation of a field and invested in intense intellectual work. To that end, the following practical lessons and theory are offered as examples that may help other teachers to grow their own practice.

A major criticism of this philosophy will surely be that teachers do not have the time to be content area experts and that school districts cannot carve out precious minutes for content area contemplation. Yet, teachers all too often have time for coaching, club sponsorship, and other activities. Perhaps educators should not be expected to engage in so many activities that do not enhance classroom practice.

The following lessons, by design, contain a measure of redundancy. Please remember the purpose here is not just to convey information, but to teach for mastery. Cognitive manipulation of material, seeing it used in different contexts, strengthens connections in the brain. The following lessons build upon themselves, finally reaching a cumulative point once the students' minds have been conceptually prepared.

And yes, this material is difficult to read and comprehend, but the process of learning involves struggle. If the alternative entails lowering learning standards with the workbook-and-study-guide-before-the-test methods, then it must be said that such methods do not actually involve learning. Students can do this.

To teachers in the field or new to the field, please hear this message from another teacher: *You are too important to not do this well.* Yes, being a content area expert and high-level classroom teacher will require total immersion in your content and your field. If you do not want to do this right, then please find something else to do. If you want to be involved in an innovative and dynamic field that will require lifelong devotion, then welcome.

THE CONNECT-THE-DOTS CURRICULUM

All probable arguments are built on the supposition, that there is in this conformity betwixt the future and the past, and therefore can never prove it. This conformity is a matter of fact, and if it must be proved, will admit of no proof but from experience. But our experience in the past can be a proof of nothing in the future. . . .—David Hume, 1740

Historiography, defined as the practice of understanding history through a thesis, has its roots in the political philosophy of George Hegel and Karl Marx. The intricacies of their historical theses need not detain us here, but their errors do remind us to proceed with caution. To practice historiography means to create a thesis about events that occurred in the past, not to make specific predictions about the future. A responsible use of historiography is essential for creating an effective history class, but a few logical parameters must first be established.

One might assume that extrapolations of broad historical trends will occur, but the idea that history is a plot with a specific and predictable ending has done as much harm to the world, in various guises, as any irrationality. This caution stated, any history class that operates without an instructor who has instilled a proper thesis to the facts merely wastes time. The facts of history must be presented behind a thesis and in the guise of a coherent narrative if a student of history is to make sense of the subject.

A good historical thesis treats the facts of history in the same way that Charles Darwin treated the facts of biology—as something to be explained through a simple and parsimonious theory that provides a framework for understanding the present but which is respectful enough of the power of randomness to make no specific predictions about the future.

To that end, the thesis presented here has to do with two major themes. The first of these themes involves the creation and storing of information. These are the facts that must be considered and synthesized for higher order thinking to occur. The second theme involves the process by which an animal evolved and refined the ability to think about and synthesize those facts while expanding its frontiers. These themes will be presented as a way of asking questions. The word "history" after all, derives from the Greek *historia*, which means to inquire.

In a connect-the-dots game, children sit down with a series of seemingly random dots on a page then, following instructions, begin to connect those points until a larger picture emerges. In the shown presented here, the "dots" are the presented facts, the teacher provides the instructions (but must first see the picture himself), and the student makes the connections. In this way, students participate in the process of compiling information and thinking, which mirrors the historical narrative.

Below, a theory of historiography is presented and five examples of "connect-the-dots" lessons are presented. The lessons themselves represent the beginnings of a set of lessons, all of which reflect the themes presented in the historiography. The purpose here is not to create a textbook of lessons based upon the connect-the-dots method, but merely to give practical examples of how the philosophy presented here can be quickly adapted for classroom use. Teachers should see these lessons not as a complete system to be thoughtlessly implemented, but as an invitation to participate in a similar endeavor.

INFORMATION THEORY: A HISTORIOGRAPHICAL THESIS FOR WORLD HISTORY

It is not the amount of knowledge that makes a brain. It is not even the distribution of knowledge. It is the interconnectedness. —Gleick, 2011

Before we condemn the Indians of this continent as wanting genius, we must consider that letters have not yet been introduced among them. Were we to compare them in their present stated with Europeans North of the Alps, when the Roman arms and arts first crossed those mountains, the comparison would be unequal, because, at that time, those parts of Europe were swarming with numbers; because numbers produce emulation, and multiply the chances of improvement, and one improvement begets another. —Jefferson, 1787

Information Theory argues that the trend of history has been toward greater and greater accretions of information, even to the point at which virtually anything can be converted into information. When paleontologists, for example, discover an ancient set of dinosaur bones, those bones are converted into information about dinosaur life. Information began with DNA, which carried instructions about how to "build" an organism, then was transferred (among humans) into spoken language, then written language, then made more accessible via translations and the evolution of paper and the printing press.

This process continues today as information is translated into binary code, stored in cyberspace, and accessed via any number of ever-changing doodads. The compilation, transmission, and translation of information provides a fascinating thesis for any history course.

Much of early history involves ideas and peoples growing up in isolation. When those peoples come into contact, through trade or war, something interesting happens. Viruses, of course, will spread. Some people will be conquered and some will intertwine, but the most interesting thing to occur is *cultural synthesis*. This is where the ideas of two cultures combine.

Often, an isolated culture will discover an invention that, when acquired by another culture, will be combined with another new invention to have a new purpose. Or, the new society will find a new and different use for the invention of the society it has just come into contact with.

For an agricultural tribe, a sharp stick may be a good way to dig ditches for irrigation. For a warlike tribe, the same stick looks like a spear. If that warlike tribe has iron jewelry, they might find that the iron jewelry, combined with the sharp digging stick, makes for a new and powerful weapon.

Most of early history is a compilation of isolated peoples who are brought together by either conquest or trade; a "glory" period then follows as the two or more cultures are synthesized and become more complex. Most of this happened in Eurasia, and, therefore, most of the early civilizations and the process of technological growth occurred there.

Cultural synthesis, the blending of cultures, technology, and ideas, can work in a number of ways. An invention may have multiple uses, but as long as it stays in one culture it will likely only be seen to have one use. For example, the Chinese invention of gunpowder was used primarily for fireworks and a few low-grade pyrotechnic weapons while it was confined to China. When the invention diffused westward, it combined with the church-bell making technology of Europe and became the bombast.

The relatively settled Chinese Empire of the Song Dynasty, the time and place in which gunpowder was invented, did not necessarily see the military potential of gunpowder. In other words, there is enormous importance in having a new set of eyes, from a culture with a new set of needs, look at an idea or invention.

There are also cases in which only a few of the necessary but insufficient causes for an invention's use are present. China, for example, had a very old pictographic language that, for the time in which it was invented, was very sophisticated. However, the massive Chinese alphabet made it impossible for the Chinese to effectively use the block printing process that was invented, like gunpowder, during the Song Dynasty.

When block printing moved westward, it encountered two other necessary (although in themselves insufficient) causes for it to become important: a small phonetic alphabet and the skill of metal working. Once Europe acquired the printing press, the Chinese became like a company that had invested all of its resources on the best early computer technology and found itself too broke to invest later, when the technology improved. They were stuck with a DOS system of language while Europe moved on to Windows.

There are also cases in which a culture evolves a stultifying form of conservatism, the kind that views new ideas and inventions as dangerous to the existing order. In the late 15th century, the Ottoman sultan Bayezid II banned the printing press, and, in 1515, this order was reiterated and the death penalty instituted for offenders.

The most important piece of technology to evolve in Eurasia in the 15th, 16th, and 17th centuries therefore skipped over the largest power in Eurasia at that time, thus facilitating an explosion of intellectual and technological growth (and, it should be said, religious war) in Western Europe.

Likewise, certain cultural factors can inhibit intellectual progress. The Romans, after stomping out the Hellenistic era (killing the irreplaceable Archimedes in the process) destroyed Western mathematics for centuries by instituting their Roman numeral system. In all their history, the Romans produced no mathematicians. Their intellectual geography no more facilitated the development of mathematical genius than the physical geography of Indiana facilitates the development of championship surfers.

Once the concept of cultural synthesis is understood, it can be applied to answer a staggering number of historical questions and to provide a framework for the development of historiography. Here is the general pattern of early history:

1. At first, civilizations grew (as far as their geography would allow) separately from each other.

2. Once one civilization gained the ability to move and conquer, then other civilizations began to synthesize.
3. Much of early world history is the story of a period of conquest, in which civilizations are joined, followed by a period of synthesis.

The second concept that needs to be understood is the importance of history itself, or the compilation of history. It is called the "Shoulders of Giants" principle, or the SOG principle, after a quote from Isaac Newton, who wrote "if I have seen farther, it is by standing on the shoulders of giants." Newton was a complex man, but this phrase is often taken to mean that Newton would not have been able to make his intellectual leaps unless scientists and mathematicians prior to him had made other discoveries, thereby allowing him to stand upon their knowledge and see farther.

No inventor or thinker works alone; he must combine and add to all of the acquired knowledge that has been discovered previously. Newton, for example, was able to work with the 0–9 number system we all know so well. If he had had worse tools, say Roman numerals, to work with, his mathematical contributions would never have been made. He was a genius because he had a personal library with all of the mathematical thought of the previous generations written in it. So, the SOG principle deals with the recording and accumulation of knowledge.

The bibliography of any work of nonfiction contains dozens or hundreds of sources. Each of those sources was itself a book composed of dozens or hundreds of other sources that were connected together and made into a new synthesis. That book will itself, one day, become just a part of somebody else's larger book. It is by this process that the shoulders we stand on get higher and higher. Of course, the accumulation of knowledge—the building of shoulders—requires that knowledge find a way to survive beyond the generation in which it was conceived.

The historiography of a world history class consists of studying how settled civilizations began, how each civilization grew up more or less separately from one another in the ancient world, and then how those civilizations began to combine or synthesize. Civilization itself grew first in the Middle East, then spread east and west, going wherever wheat grows (more on this later), except in China, where it grew along the same patterns but separately. If each civilization is a "dot," then each of these civilizations remains mostly separate and unconnected from the others.

Because humanity was separated for so long, each "dot" of a civilization developed its own language, which presented difficulties when trying to build history. Someone who speaks only Arabic will not be able to study a philosophy written in Latin and vice versa. Therefore, some of the most important people in the world were scholars who acted as translators from one language to another. Once the world's knowledge is translated into a particular culture's language, there inevitably results a period of artistic and scientific achievement in that culture simply because there are now "shoulders" for the scholars of that culture to stand on.

The next phase in world history is the connection of these "dots," in which civilizations come into contact with one another through trade or conquest. This process of conquest and synthesis began in earnest with Alexander the Great, who brought together the Persian, Egyptian, Indian, and Greek cultures. The spears that Alexander's soldiers, arranged into phalanxes, carried may as well have been large pencils by which the "dots" of earliest civilizations were connected. Flowers sprouted on Alexander's grave as the cultures he combined gave rise to the Hellenistic era, which produced a number of important thinkers, most notably Euclid and Archimedes.

The Romans expanded further, drawing lines of connections between dots with their armies. Then the Arab Muslims conquered a vast territory and translated the world's knowledge into Arabic (writing on the invention of paper, the secret for which they coerced from some captured Chinese). Then the Mongols led by Genghis Khan broke open the Chinese vase of the Song Dynasty and released gunpowder, the secret of magnetism, and the printing press to the world. The great empires of the world were all in Eurasia, where not only ideas were spreading but also diseases, which culled those with weak immune systems. Over the centuries, Eurasia became a super-continent, in which cultures combined in a new synthesis.

All areas that were isolated from this process, like Haiti, South America, Australia, and North America, fell far behind in terms of technology. The immune systems of the indigenous people were also unfortunately weak as a result of their civilizations having been lacking in disease-bearing domesticated animals.

In Eurasia and parts of Africa, several generations of humans had been shaped by arms races between the human immune system and a variety of diseases that originated with domesticated livestock. Natives of isolated regions, having gone through no such process, lacked natural protections against hyperevolved Eurasian viruses and bacteria.

Europe, a backwater since the fall of the Roman Empire (around 476 CE), was to become a beneficiary of what seemed to be the constant westward movement of ideas. As ideas and inventions trickled westward, Europe slowly began to float above her post-Roman era low water mark. When Constantinople, the dam through which Eastern ideas passed into the West, broke in 1453 (brought down by the bombast, which would soon [less than forty years later] be in the hands of Ferdinand and Isabella of Spain, who would put it to devastating use against Spain's Muslim Moors), Europe was flooded with enough ideas to raise its technological level to the point that it was possible to sail on this tide to new worlds.

DEFINITIONS

Cultural Synthesis: A biological concept extrapolated to the evolution of technology. In biology, traits that evolve for one purpose often turn out to have another, sometimes almost unrelated use when the organism moves into a new environment or when the trait combines with another separately evolved trait. Complexity grows in such a way.

Shoulders of Giants Principle: Isaac Newton famously wrote that if he'd seen farther, it was because he'd "stood on the shoulders of giants." The brain, as detailed earlier, needs to have information in order to think. The compilation and storage of information made it possible for thinkers to study, understand, and connect facts into greater levels of understanding.

SEVEN

Lesson One: Human Migration

The intent of Lesson One is to help students see connections in order to "solve" historical puzzles about the nature of early human migration. Equally as important, students should immediately get the impression that anthropology and history are not fields with totally agreed upon narratives. Scientists and historians engage in the work of presenting theories based upon the best evidence, and the ability to assess and analyze theories is a crucial part of critical thinking.

For the teacher, the lessons below indicate how information from various sources can be linked together. Once the teacher has found a pattern in the scholarship he or she is studying, it then becomes possible to plot a course for the students.

DOT 1: HUMANITY, OFF AND RUNNING

Since 1980, an innkeeper in Wales named Llanwrtyd Wells has staged a unique kind of marathon. In this race, humans run against horses over a twenty-two-mile course, through trails and across the countryside. Granted, the horses have riders on them (a necessity if they are to be taken in a specific direction), but they also have more legs than the humans do. In June 2004, a human being won the race for the first time.

It is likely that humans and horses are the only animals in nature who *could* race over long distances. Both animals are uniquely suited for long-distance running. We both have a cooling system that is quite different from any other creature in the animal kingdom: We sweat in great quantities. Sweating profusely is a phenomenon found really only twice in nature (hippos secrete a reddish sweat, but it's not very effective), but it is certainly the most efficient form of cooling that evolution has produced.

To illustrate this, imagine playing with a dog on a hot summer day. While you sweat, you remain relatively comfortable. The dog, on the other hand, will pant and likely decide to find a bowl of water or just lie down in the shade. Why? Your ancestors evolved in the brutal heat of equatorial Africa, and his (the wolf) evolved in colder northern climates. Your dog's cooling system is not nearly as effective as yours. On the other hand, see who can lie naked in the snow longer.

In the May 2006 issue of *Discover* magazine, in an article titled *Born to Run*, writer Ingfei Chin outlines the hypothesis of two professors. The first is Dennis Bramble, a biologist at the University of Utah, and the other, Daniel Lieberman, is a paleoanthropologist at Harvard. These two men have come up with a novel theory of one reason why humans may have been effective hunters.

In brief, human beings are the animal kingdom's most effective endurance runners. A human in great shape can outlast a horse, and the article claims that "under the right conditions, [humans] can also outrun just about any other animal on the planet—including dogs, wolves, hyenas, and antelope, the other great endurance runners."

The scientists claim that human beings are structured for running. The *Discover* article states: "From our abundant sweat glands to our Achilles tendons, from our big knee joints to our muscular glutei maximi (the behind), human bodies are beautifully toned running machines" (Chin 2006).

According to these scientists, humans get rid of heat by sweating through millions of sweat glands whereas most animals have to pant. Sweating is a much more effective method of cooling. Humans also lack fur and that helps us to cool down as well.

In a strange experiment, especially for the big cat, Harvard biologists inserted a rectal thermometer into a cheetah (I'm assuming that safety equipment was worn) and put the cat on a treadmill. When the cheetah's temperature reached 105 degrees, it quit running. Cheetahs, obviously, can outrun humans in a sprint. But over the long haul, it's no contest.

The professors also point out that the existence of a piece of anatomy called the *nuchal ligament*, described as "a tendonlike band that links the head to the spine." All running animals, like horses, dogs, and rabbits, have the ligament. It is used to keep the head steady while running. Humans have a type of this band on our spines as well.

In fossils and old bones, one can see where the ligament would have been because it is attached to a ridge at the base of the human skull. *Homo erectus*, a human cousin for 2 million years, has the ridge. But older hominids, like australopithecine, who went extinct about 4.4 million years ago, do not have the ridge. This means that the nuchal ligament, which holds the head steady while running, evolved in more modern humans. Human beings also have big tendons in our legs. These tendons are not necessary for walking, but the heavy bouncing of running long distances requires them.

Now, long-distance running could not have evolved as a mechanism to *escape* predators. It does no good to be able to outrun a cheetah over five miles when the cat can knock you over in the first fifty feet. So it must have had another purpose, and here is where this theory gets interesting. The *Discover* article claims: "Bramble and Lieberman find it conceivable that endurance running helped hunters pursue prey to exhaustion."

Human hunters may have run animals to exhaustion and then killed them.

An example is cited. In the Kalahari Desert of Botswana (southern Africa), Bushmen chase down kudu antelope. The hunters only run after the antelope when the temperature is over 100 degrees Fahrenheit. The Bushmen hunt in the following way: 1. To prepare for the hunt, they gulp down water. 2. Two men chase the animal, tracking it and staying on its trail. 3. One hunter hangs back and conserves his energy. 4. The first two men fall back. 5. The third man, the one going more slowly, rushes forward when the animal is exhausted and overheated, then he spears the animal.

Meat is then be taken back to the tribe. Lieberman watched the men hunt and clocked them at speeds of 4 to 6 miles per hour, at which they ran between 2 and 6 ½ hours. They had to run upward of 22 miles to kill their prey. In comparison, the fastest marathon runners can go 26 miles at 12 miles per hour.

The Lieberman-Bramble hypothesis is a new theory that has not yet been through the rigors of thorough scientific testing, but it is an intriguing hypothesis. Perhaps our ability to run, combined with another unique talent for throwing, is what allowed human hunters to survive and flourish long enough to decimate animal populations in North America and elsewhere.

DOT 2: KEEPING COOL

In his book *Africa: The Biography of a Continent*, John Reader points out that human beings, like planet Earth, are made up of 70% water. He claims that "The water content of a healthy 65 kg human is nearly 50 litres—enough to fill 150 Coca-Cola cans" (1997, p. 83).

We'll forgive his use of the anti-American metric system and just take from this the lesson that humans are in dire need of water. He also claims, again in metrics, that:

"The average person, in average temperature conditions, must take in and excrete about 2.5 litres of liquid each day (amounting to the replacement of about 5 percent of total water content)." (p. 83)

Thus, human beings need to ingest a lot of water in order to stay cool, since our bodies generate enormous amounts of heat. Reader mentions that by just sitting and doing nothing you're putting out as much energy as a 75-watt electric bulb! So, it's no accident that early humans tended to settle near water.

Because our ancestors evolved in the heat of Eastern Africa, it was important for them to have effective cooling systems. As stated in Dot 1, humans are one of the only species who can run effectively over long distances. To be able to run in heat means that an incredibly efficient body cooling system is necessary, and, as Reader writes: "We have the most effective body cooling system of any living mammal" (p. 86).

Not only that, but the fact that humans stand upright helps us to avoid the sun's heat. Reader quotes a thesis by Pete Wheeler that showed that: "by standing upright, the bipedal hominids avoided 60 percent of the direct solar radiation to which they would have been exposed as quadrupeds" (p. 87).

According to Wheeler, and as explained by Reader, human ancestors who walked upright could stop being so hairy all over. Fur is actually good protection against sunlight, but it requires energy to make thick hair, and evolution doesn't favor wasted energy. It was only necessary for our ancestors to have hair on their heads and shoulders. After all, the sun was only regularly hitting those parts. We didn't really lose hair, by the way, it's just that the hairs got thinner. Reader points out that, by the square centimeter, modern humans have the same *amount* of hair as a chimpanzee—ours just aren't as thick.

Anyway, the point being that our bodies are remarkably adapted to shed heat—for the most part. We'll see some slight exceptions in a moment.

DOT 3: BIG BRAINS

According to Reader, the ability to cool easily gave our prehuman ancestors what he calls "an exceptional degree of body-temperature stability" while the brains of our ancestors were still small. However, this body cooling system allowed the human brain to evolve to a much larger size. Or, as he puts it: "thus coincidentally established the precise conditions which favored the evolution of *the* most definitive human characteristic: the large cognitive brain" (p. 89).

The cooling systems of other animals involve sending blood to the brain and back to the nose, which is why the nose of a healthy dog (and of most animals) is wet. This system cools the brain, but allows the body to heat up.

Since we cool differently and more efficiently, it was possible for our brains to grow larger. Reader writes about the brain: " Brain is 'expensive tissue.' The modern human brain is six times larger than that of a typical mammal of comparable size . . . it consumes over 16 percent of the body's energy budget" (p. 89).

Wheeler, whose thesis Reader is quoting, ended his work with these words: "'It is probably no coincidence,' Wheeler concludes, 'that today the mammal with the most highly developed brain and social behavior is the species which possesses the most elaborate cooling system'" (p. 90).

DOT 4: OUT OF AFRICA TWICE

Okay, so now we've explained much of how our prehuman ancestors were physically prepared to settle about the world. It would be nice if humans just evolved in Africa and then moved out from there, but, as is usually the case, the story is much more complicated than that.

It turns out that the first migrations were undertaken by human ancestors. And, to begin explaining the history of human migration, we must go to the place where humanity first emerged: Africa. In the September 2005 issue of *National Geographic*, in an article entitled *The Shape of Africa*, Jared Diamond wrote this:

> As to its human history, [Africa] is the place where some seven million years ago the evolutionary lines of apes and protohumans diverged. It remained the only continent our ancestors inhabited until around two million years ago, when *Homo erectus* expanded out of Africa into Europe and Asia. Over the next 1.5 million years the populations of those three continents followed such different evolutionary courses that they became distinct species. Europe's became the Neandertals, Asia's remained *Homo erectus*, but Africa's evolved into our own species, *Homo sapiens*, which means "wise man." Modern humans are referred to as *Homo sapiens sapiens* or "wise, wise man." (You get titles like that when species name themselves.)

First of all, you might be asking how we knew when *Homo sapiens* became *Homo sapiens sapiens*. Don't fall into the trap of thinking that one human was born from caveman-like parents. Again, the hardest questions in biology involves drawing lines and saying "here is where a new species begins." The first totally modern humans wouldn't have looked any different from all of the other prehumans they were living with.

Back to Africa: What this means is that there was a human ancestor living 1.5 million years ago. A group of these prehumans left Africa. Some settled in Europe, and some settled in Asia. Over a long period of time, given the different environmental pressures, they began to evolve into three distinct species. The group that stayed home in Africa became modern humans like you and me. These modern humans then left Africa. The Neandertals of Europe, and Peking Man, as the Asian species became known, would have been perfectly happy if modern humans would have just stayed put, given what happens next. Diamond writes:

> Sometime between 10,000 and 50,000 years ago our African ancestors underwent further profound change. Whether it was the development of complex speech or something else, such as a change in brain wiring, we aren't sure. Whatever it was, it transformed those early *Homo sapiens* into what paleoanthropologists call "behaviorally modern" *Homo sapiens*. Those people, probably with brains similar to our own, expanded again into Europe and Asia. Once there, they exterminated or replaced or interbred with Neandertals and Asia's hominims and became the dominant human species throughout the world.

Homo sapiens might have killed them all or simply outcompeted them for resources. Recent DNA evidence confirms that a certain amount of interbreeding must have occurred between humans and Neandertals. We don't know what happened to our evolutionary cousins, but I will say this: The history of humanity from its earliest recorded days seems to be one of movement and conquest. One group of people, usually living in a society connected to others, moves outward for some reason and then conquers the other peoples it finds. It's almost always the people moving who conquer (or, in the case of the Ming Chinese, achieve dominance.) Why? If they're moving, they probably need something, and if they have the ability *to move*, they've probably developed the technology necessary *to conquer*.

It is important to note that it doesn't appear that either Neandertals or Peking Man were our direct ancestors. Instead, we all three shared a common ancestor, *Homo erectus*. Imagine putting a few of a certain type of bird on three different islands and leaving them alone for 1.5 million years. When future scientists returned to study the islands in their flying cars, there would be three different types of bird (for simplicity's sake we'll say three; there might be a whole bunch more), one on each island, but all would share the common ancestor of the type that you dropped off there earlier.

DOT 5: NORTH AMERICAN ANIMALS EVOLVE LARGE SIZE

Evolution often favors size, and many North American animals, such as the woolly mammoth and several types of "monsters," evolved accordingly large bodies. Millions of years of evolution favored large size in these animals. The big and the strong won fights and therefore mating rights.

North America was, at one time, the home of a variety of towering animals. Visit any museum and you will be astonished at the stuffed recreation of an ancient giant beaver. Its sheer size is amazing, especially when compared to the tiny animals we are used to seeing today. Years of animal evolution in a North America that was free from humans (who were still busy migrating out of Africa) had led to an evolutionary race for size.

In *Third Chimpanzee* (1992), Diamond writes:

> When Indian hunters arrived, they found the Americas teeming with big mammals that are now extinct: elephantlike mammoths and mastadonts, ground sloths weighing up to three tons, armadillolike glyptodonts weighing up to one tone, bear-sized beavers, and sabertooth cats, plus American lions, cheetahs, camels, horses, and many others.

All of these animals were quickly exterminated. Why? Archaeological evidence indicates that these animals died out when humans arrived. Big animals on other continents died out when humans arrived as well. What was happening?

DOT 6: THE HUMAN ABILITY TO THROW

In Alfred Crosby's book, *Throwing Fire* (2002), Crosby highlights research that shows that human beings are the only animals who can throw. According to Crosby, the human ability to rotate our shoulders and throw things may have been the singular factor in the development of our large brains, and quite possibly could explain our rise to dominance over the macro-animals of our planet. Crosby's book draws a line showing how human beings and our evolutionary predecessors have constantly tried to build upon our ability to throw, at first using *atlatls* (wooden objects that held a dart and gave humans a few extra "joints," which in turn allowed them to whip the dart at greater velocities), then arrows, catapults, guns, rockets, nuclear weapons, and so forth.

Crosby states:

> The ability to throw, to commit violence at a distance with rock, spear, javelin, dart, and arrow, transformed hominids from prey to predator and made them the first creatures of size who could effect change at a distance. That equipped them to survive and exploit even the largest land animals. (p. 15)

The ability to throw coupled nicely with the sight mechanisms that Australopithecines developed while living among trees, where sight and depth perception (important for "tree traveling" as Crosby puts it) outmaneuvered the sense of smell in the evolution of our human predecessors (p. 18).

The combination of this depth perception, along with the ability to throw, made later humans a suddenly powerful adversary. A life among trees, according to Crosby, would have helped our predecessor, the Australopithecine, to do more than just develop sight and depth perception, but also the shoulder.

Crosby notes that the Australopithecine "had, like their ape relatives, upper limb structures (collarbones and ball-and-socket shoulders) that enabled them to revolve their arms in full circles. . . . They can throw overhand pretty well if they want to" (p. 19).

So, the tree-life developed in our ancestors both a sense of depth perception and the rotating shoulder, which likely came about to use in branch-swinging, not throwing. But tree-life had more gifts to give the Australopithecine, in this case, our much celebrated thumb:

> At the far, the distal, end of the Australopithecines' remarkable arms were the stunningly versatile primate hand, quite like our own, "the narrowest hinge" of which, according to Walt Whitman, "puts to scorn all machinery." The Australopithecine's thumb, nearly as opposable to the fingers and full palms as ours, was powerful and yet dexterous, capable of instantly cooperating with the fingers in any number of kinds of grips, including, in all probability, the three-jawed chuck grip favored by baseball pitchers. (p. 19)

So, Australopithecines developed the shoulder, hand, and visual depth perception necessary for throwing not because of the advantages that it gave for hunting or defense, but for the advantages it gave for swinging through trees. Once these creatures moved from the trees to the ground, they likely discovered that they had been unwittingly equipped with the means for their own survival—and later dominance—among the more physically powerful macro-animals of the world. A set of incidents that Crosby states was "a metamorphosis as wonderful as that of dinosaur feathers, probably evolved for warmth or display, becoming bird feathers for flight" (p. 21).

The unique human capacity for throwing evolved rapidly into a successful method of hunting and defense. Crosby points out that "A good baseball pitcher or cricket bowler can throw a ball (a sort of manufactured rock) at velocities as high or higher than 90 miles or 140 kilometers an hour. The impact of a missile at such velocities can crack ribs or even skulls. The impact of a dozen or so all at once would at the very least be discouraging" (p. 27).

All in all, the human ability to throw is a remarkable evolutionary "achievement" by any standard. We are regaled sometimes, by biologists or writers who like to point out how fragile modern humans would be in a completely natural environment. Our brains, not our physical fighting or hunting skills, are what have allowed us to survive and flourish. This kind of argument neglects to explain just how exactly it was that humans survived such harsh biological climates to grow big brains in the first place. As Crosby writes:

> In order to throw a missile and hit a target the size of a rabbit at four meters, I must release the missile within a duration, "a launch window" of *eleven milliseconds*. That act, which most of us can perform some of the time and some of us all of the time, is in the same category of natural miracles as a bat's ability to snatch insects out of the dark guided by echolocation. (pp. 22–23)

This ability to throw was helped along by human ingenuity. The creation of a device called the *atlatl*, which was a long stick with a single joint that held a large dart, signaled what was perhaps "the first human device with two moving parts" (p. 34).

This device, obviously, allowed a human to whip a dart with greater velocity, thus upping the human's killing capacity. The *atlatl* is important not just because it greatly empowered human hunters, but also because it marks a point at which humans had intellectually "outgrown" evolution in a way. Instead of having to wait long periods of time for nature to select powerful throwing arms with added joints, humans simply *built* an extra joint, adding to their own innate capacities. Humans had moved in many ways away from the evolution of the body to the evolution of the mind, where competition for survival would depend on ideas.

CONNECTING THE DOTS: BLITZKRIEG THEORY

According to Crosby, the human ability to throw may help to explain why it was that so many large animals in North America died out around the time of human migration. (Our capacity for throwing may also explain why dogs like to play fetch. My German shepherd, Gus, may only bring back the stick after I throw it because he wants to see me do it again . . . . I'm kidding.)

The ability to throw was an evolutionary factor that, as it turns out, was tantamount to a jackpot for humans when they reached the North American continent by whatever means (I'll not jump into the controversy about how humans got to North America) simply because these big animals had evolved right into the hands of human hunters.

Simply put, there's a lot of steak on a woolly mammoth. The big animals, who had evolved to fight other big animals, were suddenly no longer so powerful against the scrawny bipeds who were tossing pointy things of various shapes and sizes into their sides. Humans had evolved, in trees, the anatomical equipment needed to throw. Many North American animals had evolved the ability to be big, meaty, and slow. Humans and their rotator cuffs represented nothing short of a biological invasion on an unprepared ecosystem. The human ability to throw likely led to the extinction of many large animals, as human hunters easily picked off the massive prehistoric animals and left only the smaller, faster animals that could get away from humans regularly enough to reproduce. With the big prey animals gone, their predators, like the sabertooth tiger, also died out, from lack of food.

The idea that human hunters quickly wiped out the large animals is sometimes called the "blitzkrieg" theory, or, my favorite name, the "black hole" theory since these animals likely disappeared into the "black holes" of human mouths.

At the end of this lesson, students should be able to understand basic biological concepts and explain the best modern theories as to how humans spread across the globe and why large animals plunged into extinction whenever humans arrived. Testing would involve having students analyze a primary document or answering a question using the information they have manipulated in class. For example, students might be presented with this prompt and a quote from Jared Diamond:

> Read the following quote and, in your essay explain, using the theories studied in class, why *Homo sapiens* were likely so successful in settling around the world. Use quotes from the excerpt in your answer.
>
> *Sometime between 10,000 and 50,000 years ago, our African ancestors underwent further profound change. Whether it was the development of complex speech or something else, such as a change in brain wiring, we aren't sure. Whatever it was, it transformed those early* Homo sapiens *into what paleoanthropologists call "behaviorally modern"* Homo sapiens. *Those people, probably with brains similar to our own, expanded again into Europe and Asia. Once there, they exterminated or replaced or interbred with Neandertals and Asia's hominims and became the dominant human species throughout the world.*

To answer such a question, students must be able to exhibit a high level of reading comprehension and also be able to analyze and synthesize the various theories presented in class. This may seem difficult—and it is— but students at the secondary level are not expected to turn in the kind of answers one would expect from a graduate student. The point is to have students work, engage in a process of real learning, and stretch their skills.

EIGHT

Lesson Two: Assessment for Historical Pattern Recognition

Not all lessons need involve connections between deep works of scholarship. Often, a lesson can simply present students with text for the purpose assessing whether or not they can draw connections, see patterns, and think thematically. In other words, can the students engage in the same kind of thinking that the teacher has to when preparing lessons? The following example of an assessment tests this ability.

FINDING PATTERNS IN HISTORY

In Paul Cartledge's book *The Spartans*, Cartledge wrote about a Spartan defeat during the Peloponnesian War:

Quote I

> [I]n the seventh year of the War, in 425. Incredible news reached the outside world of an extraordinary happening on Sphacteria, a small island just off the south-west coast of Messenia and within Sparta's home territory. A 400 strong force of Spartan and Perioecic hoplites, including 120 of the Homoioi or Peers, had surrendered there following a twelve-week blockade by Athenian forces aided by descendants of former Messenian Helots. This event shook the Greek world. It simply was not supposed to happen. For it contradicted absolutely the Spartan myth, as laid down and exemplified most famously at Thermopylae, the myth of Never Surrender . . . .
>
> To the Greeks as a whole, and to the Spartans in particular, it was inconceivable that 120 products of the Agoge education system would surrender after a mere eighty days of privation, thirst and hunger.

65

When questioned about that very fact, one of the prisoners in Athens is said to have given as his reason for surrendering that he hadn't been involved in a fair fight, man to man. He hadn't been fighting against true men in regular warfare using masculine weapons. Instead, he had been brought low by what he called the enemies' "spindles," which he claimed were incapable of distinguishing a true warrior from a born coward. The reference of "spindles," Thucydides explains, was to arrows—ignoble, cowardly, long-distance weapons, typically womanish. (p. 35)

Quote II

A single one of us can defeat your whole army. If you do not believe it, you may try, only please order your army to stop shooting with firearms. (An unnamed Mamluk emir, prisoner to Selim the Grim, Ottoman Sultan, after the battle of Marjdabik 1516)

Quote III

Victory did not come to the one who played by the rules; it came to the one who made the rules and imposed them on his enemy. (Jack Weatherford, p. 56)

ASSIGNED ESSAY

Compare quotes I and II. The Spartans and the Arabs, separated by two thousand years, are lamenting the same problem. Once you understand the quotes, explain what Dr. Weatherford means in quote III. Include the comparison and all the other criteria for an essay in your answer.

NINE

Lesson Three: Historical Paradigm Shift

Thomas Kuhn's concept of a paradigm shift, detailed in his classic work *The Structure of Scientific Revolutions* (1996), may be overused now in public discourse. Kuhn never meant for the phrase to be applied to new forms of economic policy, for example. Instead, Kuhn questioned how it was that scientific models of the universe could change from one generation to the next. This process, as noted by the astrophysicist and historian John Gribbin (2004), typically is facilitated by technological evolution.

Galileo facilitated a paradigm shift by observing the moons of Jupiter, yet millions of people had viewed Jupiter prior to Galileo; however, none of them had the privilege of doing so with the extra help of a telescope. What Galileo saw forced a rethinking of the geocentric model of the solar system, and a total shift in the way that people saw the universe and their place in it constituted a scientific paradigm shift.

Study of this historical process, of course, can lead to an epistemological crisis, as it brings into question the validity of current historical paradigms. These questions have been answered by model-dependent realism (MDR) but need not bog down the narrative here. In the lesson below, the concept of the paradigm shift, put into historical context, is broken down for students to explore. The lesson is included here to indicate that even the most complex ideas can be simplified for student understanding.

DOT 1: EUROPEAN MINDS AT THE OUTSET OF THE MEDIEVAL PERIOD

By the Medieval era, Europeans appear on the periphery as a group to be conquered or, on occasion, to win a battle and prevent the far western part of the continent from being overrun by Muslims or Mongols. At least, that's pretty much how it seemed to the "civilized" world then. It may be strange to think about now, but during the cultural flowering of the Chinese, Muslim, and Mongol worlds, Europe was considered a backwater.

In his great book *The Measure of Reality*, Alfred Crosby (1997) sums up the European situation:

> In the mid-ninth century CE Ibn Khurradadhbeh described Western Europe as a source of "eunuchs, slave girls and boys, brocade, beavers skins, glue, sables and swords," and not much more. A century later another Muslim geographer, the great Masudi, wrote that Europeans were dull in mind and heavy in speech, and that "farther they are to the north the more stupid, gross, and brutish they are." This was what any Muslim sophisticate would have expected of Christians, particularly the "Franks," as Western Europeans were known to the Islamic world, because these people, barbarians most of them, lived at the remote Atlantic margin of Eurasia, far from the heartlands of its high cultures. (p. 3)

The interesting thing is that these European barbarians would, in an incredibly short time, be running the worldwide show like no other empire before them. This is by no means to say that their eventual ruling of the world would be entirely a good thing, but it is a fascinating rise, and it poses a lot of great questions. As Crosby says:

> Six centuries later the Franks were at least equal to, and even ahead of, the Muslims and everyone else in the world in certain kinds of mathematics and mechanical innovation. They were in the first stage of developing science-cum-technology that would be the glory of their civilization and the edged weapon of their imperialistic expansion. How, between the ninth and sixteenth centuries, had these bumpkins managed all that? (p. 5)

For Muslim civilization, this rise of Western Europe came as quite a shock. The Arabs were used to thinking of themselves as on top of the world. Arabic and Persian were the languages of the elite. Islam was the religion of culture. In his famous book *What Went Wrong*, Bernard Lewis writes of the Islamic attitude:

> For most medieval Muslims, Christendom meant, primarily, the Byzantine Empire, which gradually became smaller and weaker until its final disappearance with the Turkish conquest of Constantinople in 1453. The remoter lands of Europe were seen in much the same light as

the remoter lands of Africa—as an outer darkness of barbarism and unbelief from which there was nothing to learn and little even to be imported, except slaves and raw materials. For both the northern and southern barbarians, their best hope was to be incorporated in the empire of the caliphs, and thus attain the benefits of religion and civilization. (p. 4)

As Europe rose, the true question for the Muslims was "What went wrong?" However, our attention will now turn to Europe, where the question we will be asking about the barbaric tribes in the outer darkness will be "What went right?"

It could be that the West rose precisely because it had no clear direction for so long. It had not calcified into a certain belief system. It was not unified but was perfectly prepared to take all of the fruits of the other unified civilizations and use them and their combinations to grow. As Crosby states:

Yet the West, compared with contemporary Muslim, Indian, and Chinese civilizations, was uniquely prepared to survive and even profit from such an avalanche of change. Western Europe had the characteristics that physicians seeking means to counter the disorder of senescence hope to find in fetal tissue, that is to say, not so much vigor per se, though that is surely valuable in itself, as a lack of differentiation. Fetal tissue is so young that it retains the potentiality for becoming whatever kind of tissue is required. (p. 53)

Stem cells are important for scientific research because they have the potential to become any kind of tissue, but once the cell has "decided" what kind of tissue it wants to be (say, skin tissue, or heart, or spinal cord), then there's no turning back. The civilizations of the East had already "decided" and were unable to deal with changes. Europe could still be whatever it wanted, and when ideas flooded into it like nutrient-rich blood, it grew in a hurry.

Europe may have been the place in the best position to deal with a sudden *paradigm shift*, or shift in way of viewing the world. Let's explore this notion with a story.

DOT 2: CONCEPT OF THE PARADIGM SHIFT, A STORY

Dr. Avery was an explorer in the 1950s. He was a professor of indigenous cultures at Oxford, in England, and traveled extensively in deep forests and jungles looking to make first contact with "untouched tribes" or tribes that had never had contact with the outside world. It was Dr. Avery's belief that there were tribes of people in the world who, since they were not pressured by environmental changes, would be living essentially as people had since the Stone Age.

Dr. Avery traveled, with his porters, deep into the jungles of Brazil where there were rumors that one of these "untouched" tribes still lived. After several weeks of rugged travel through the jungle, one of the members of Dr. Avery's party glimpsed a young man slipping away through the trees. Excited at the prospect of being the first "civilized" man to make contact with this tribe, Dr. Avery pushed his group to track the Native.

After several hours of wandering, sometimes aimlessly, Dr. Avery and his party finally came across a small village in a clearing of the jungle. Tiny grass huts stood along the edges of the clearing and a fire pit had been dug in the center. There were no people in the village, but Dr. Avery could sense eyes on him and knew that the villagers must be hiding behind the trees, afraid, watching him.

Dr. Avery raised his hands high to show that he had no weapons, walked to the center of the village, and dropped off a bag full of beads, trinkets, small knives, and other little gifts. He then left and camped about half a mile away from the village, not wanting to frighten the Natives.

The next day, Dr. Avery, afraid that a large group would scare the villagers, took a single guide from his party and went back to the village. Immediately, he saw that his bag of gifts was gone. Furthermore, without his armed men, the villagers were not afraid of the professor any longer. In fact, many a bead-wearing woman came up to him and appeared to express their gratitude for the gifts.

It was not long before a big-bellied and broad-shouldered man came out of one of the huts. This man had very dark skin and looked powerful. He carried a club with many notches that Dr. Avery assumed represented his victories in battle. He greeted the professor with a smile, and invited him to sit on a rock, where they did the best they could to have a discussion.

Dr. Avery soon found that he was the beneficiary of two remarkable pieces of luck. The first piece of luck was that the chief seemed as interested in him as he was in the chief, which meant that they could both learn a lot from each other. Second, the chief's language was apparently very close in structure to the language of Dr. Avery's guide. Dr. Avery, being a language historian or linguist, knew that at some point his guide's family and the chief's family must have had some kind of cultural tie. Language alters and evolves over the years but retains much of its original shape.

Dr. Avery, his guide, and the chief set about breaking down the language barrier, and they did so over the following weeks. When conversation was more or less possible, Dr. Avery found himself to be in for the shock of his life.

The chief's name was Alloxio, and the name of his tribe was Paxugral-lahia, roughly translated to mean "People of the Earth." Later, when he got back to England, where he could lecture about his travels, Dr. Avery would simply call them the "Reversers."

It just so happened that the professor turned sixty years old while on the trip. His guide explained this to the chief.

"Oh, you are very young indeed," said the chief with his eyes wide. At first, Dr. Avery took this for flattery and smiled politely. But then the chief continued, "when you are old like me, there will be less to look forward to."

Dr. Avery was puzzled by this comment. The chief really was a young man, probably not yet thirty. "Old?" Dr. Avery said. He then asked how many years the man had lived.

"I don't know," the chief said. "I have about thirty left before my death."

"How do you know?" asked the professor.

"Well, I can see it."

"What?"

"Yes, I can see what's before me. I'll have a wife in five years. Then, I'll break my leg in ten years, when I fall down a hill on a hunt."

Dr. Avery was beyond shocked. He had met the chief's wife, and they were already married.

"I am much older than you," Dr. Avery said. "I've probably lived twice your years."

"No," said the chief, himself looking confused. "You just said you had sixty years of life ahead of you. Will it be a good life?"

"How would I know?"

"Can't you see it?"

Then it dawned on Dr. Avery what the confusion was. What he saw as memory, Chief Alloxio viewed as images of the future.

Alloxio soon figured out the problem as well, and an argument ensued.

"All people are born in different ways, and die the same way," Alloxio said. "Life comes to you at different times; some are shriveled and wrinkly, some are small, but as we get older, and go down life's path that is before us, we have less future in front of us. There is no, 'memory' as you call it. Those images are the future."

"That's insane!" cried the professor. "All people are born in the same way and die in different ways. You can't see the future, but you can remember the past."

"No, no, everyone lives life and has a nice peaceful death. We all get smaller and smaller until finally we go up into our mother's warm safe stomach and then dissolve into nothing."

"You really think this?"

"Of course. In fact, when people know they only have fourteen years or so left of life all they want to do is chase the opposite sex. They care nothing about anything but meeting girls or boys. Then, later, they don't even care about that. They only want to play. Then when they are very old, we can't get them to speak anymore. They don't work, only lay around. At the end, we are expected to even feed and clean up after them!"

"I don't understand your way of thinking," Dr. Avery said. "In my world, we see the images in our mind as things that have already happened and the future is unknowable. We have to teach the young, and then they become old."

"Yes, finally we agree on something! The old do have to teach the young. The young are always so concerned with the world, with arguments and wars. The old are concerned only with their next meal. The old and wise can spend a day playing in mud, or in awe of an insect. They speak if they want, play if they want, and it's important that they teach the younger generation the importance of these things."

"No, you're incorrect again," said Dr. Avery, putting his head in his hands.

"Look," said Alloxio, "when you stare at a path in the jungle that path is in *front* of you, correct?"

"Yes," replied the professor.

"Well, since what you see in your mind is in front of you, too, doesn't it make sense that it would be the future?"

Dr. Avery and Chief Alloxio argued like this for a long time, but eventually had to throw up their hands. Neither could argue that his view of a lifetime was correct. The lifetime, the images in people's minds, were what they were, but it was the way the two men from different cultures viewed them that was important.

Paradigm Shift

This story shows the radical way in which minds can view the same thing differently. It may have never occurred to you to think of the images in your mind as anything *but* memories. *Your* concept of time, like mine, is likely of a fixed line, going unstoppably forward. It is measurable, dividable, and ultimately understandable.

Please understand that the story here does not indicate a person aging backward in forward time. In Alloxio's vision, a scar is evidence that one will be cut, not that one has been cut. Think of a movie put on pause. From the single screen shot (analogous to a memory) determining whether the action is moving in forward or reverse is impossible.

If this is confusing, give your mind time to adjust, as understanding Alloxio's vision of time requires an entirely different mental model. Now you know how medieval people must have felt when they were told that the seeming solid Earth they stood was actually in motion while the seemingly mobile sun remained stable.

It may be difficult to understand that human beings have not always had the mindset that we have today. In his book, *A World Lit Only By Fire: The Medieval Mind and the Renaissance*, William Manchester describes this mindset:

> The most baffling, elusive, yet in many ways the most insignificant dimensions of the medieval mind were invisible and silent. One was the medieval man's total lack of ego. Even those with creative powers had no sense of self. Each of the great soaring medieval cathedrals, our most treasured legacy from that age, required three or four centuries to complete. Canterbury was twenty-three generations in the making. . . . Yet we know nothing of the architects or builders. They were glorifying God. To them their identity in this life was irrelevant. (p. 21)

Can you imagine a modern politician getting funding to start a project that wouldn't be complete for several hundred years? Can you imagine a modern architect not wanting to take credit for her work? Manchester goes on to point out that the vast majority of 60 million Europeans alive during that time had no last name. They didn't even name their villages. (By the way, don't get too excited if you find that your last name can be traced back to royalty. You were more likely to be a serf than a duke. In later years, the peasants took the surnames of their lords.)

News of the big events of the day rarely reached the villages of Europe. As Manchester says:

> Each hamlet was inbred, isolated, unaware of the world beyond the most familiar local landmark: a creek, or mill, or tall tree scarred by lightning. There were no newspapers or magazines to inform the common people of great events; occasional pamphlets might reach them, but they were usually theological and, like the Bible, were always published in Latin. . . . The folk (*Leute, popolo, pueblo, gens, gente*) were baptized, shriven, attended Mass, received the host at communion, married, and received the last rites never dreaming that they should be informed about great events let alone have any voice in them. (p. 22)

The people in the hamlets were illiterate, walked around naked in the hot summer, and had no concept of privacy. The medieval peasant also had no concept of skepticism. Nothing, whether it be the teachings of the Church or the way that crops were plowed, was ever questioned. They knew nothing of time as we conceive it. According to Manchester:

> In the medieval mind there was also no awareness of time, which is even more difficult to grasp. Inhabitants of the twentieth century are instinctively aware of past, present, and future. At any given moment most can quickly identify where they are on this temporal scale—the year, usually the date or day of the week, and frequently, by glancing at their wrists, the time of day. Medieval men were rarely aware of which century they were living in. There was no reason they should have been. There are great differences between everyday life in 1791

and 1991, but there were very few between 791 and 991. . . . Any innovation was inconceivable; to suggest the possibility of one would have invited suspicion, and because the accused were guilty until they had proved themselves innocent by surviving impossible ordeals—by fire, water, or combat—to be suspect was to be doomed. (p. 23)

It's a sad truth that history has never concerned itself much with the masses. Billions can live in poverty, as they do today, and yet the march of complexity can go on if the information necessary is carried only by a few. The great mass of information sent through e-mail, accessed on the web, and through newspapers, text messages, and phone calls is basically useless to history. But it only takes a very few good ideas to break through. In the Medieval period, these ideas broke through in the monasteries. One invention, especially, would change the way *everybody* thought.

DOT 3: A PERSONAL RELATIONSHIP WITH GOD AND THE MONASTERY

The collapse of the Roman Empire was, again, a very gradual thing that the average citizen probably did not even notice. However, as the Roman collapse became more and more apparent, the city states to the west began to crumble and become independent lands unto themselves, fiefdoms, ruled by royalty with expensive weapons, who lorded over peasant farmers. In Europe, the era after the fall of Rome was commonly called the "Dark Age," but few historians call it that now. It was actually a period during which a new mode of thought was germinating in Europe.

For Europe, it was the birth of the monastery that held civilization together. In *A Brief History of the Western World*, Greer and Lewis write of how the monastery came to be:

The Christian thinker Augustine developed the idea, already advanced by Paul, of the Church as a community of believers that was predestined (chosen in advance) by God for salvation, and which was independent of the fate of any empire. Christian men and women began to live a life of closeness to God and freedom from the distractions of the world as monks and nuns, providing the Church with a new elite. . . . The barbarian invaders themselves eventually adopted the Catholic beliefs of the people they had conquered. By CE 600, Christianity would have the inner strength that would enable it to survive its next great trial—the loss of countless believers in the Middle East and North Africa to the rival monotheism of Islam—to seize its next great opportunity—the spreading of the monotheist revolution to the barbarian peoples of northern Europe. (p. 164)

From Augustine, again, we see the ideas that will form the policies and ideas of the Catholic Church. The idea was that a *personal* god existed, one who spoke to people, and that it was possible, through rituals, meditation, and study, to get to know that god. The better this god was known, the better it would be for the believer. Or so it was thought.

As J. M. Roberts states:

> The end of the classical world also saw two new institutions emerge in the western Church which were to be lifelines in the dangerous rapids between a civilization which had collapsed and one yet to be born. The first was Christian monasticism, a phenomenon first appearing in the East. It was about 285 that a Copt, St. Antony, retired to a hermit's life in the Egyptian desert. His example was followed by others who watched, prayed and strove with demons or mortified the flesh by fasting and more dubious disciplines. Some of them drew together in communities. (p. 299)

However, the monastery in its most recognizable form can be credited not to St. Antony but to St. Benedict. In his book, *Medieval Lives*, Terry Jones describes (with a wit deserving of a former Monty Python star) Benedict:

> The idea of living in a community cut off from your fellow men in order to worship God didn't really get going in the West until around CE 500, when a Roman nobleman by the name of Benedict got fed up with life in the big city. Rome was far too full of people enjoying good food, drink and sex for his taste. So he took a servant and settled in the countryside where, unfortunately, his reputation for being able miraculously to mend broken pottery started to attract crowds.
>
> So he sought out a reasonably inaccessible cave halfway up a cliff face, with no modern conveniences and no plumbing. A monk from one of the nearby religious establishments came every day to lower a basket of food down to him. And Benedict made sure there was no oyster sauce or deep-fried wontons in his daily picnic—indeed, he didn't want anything he could actually enjoy. As far as Benedict was concerned, God placed us in this world to give us the opportunity to refrain from enjoying our brief time here, in order to concentrate on thanking him for placing us in this world.
>
> It was a philosophy that seems to have appealed to a surprising number of people, and news of Benedict's sanctity spread throughout the region. He ended up founding his own monastery. There he wrote his famous Rule (or set of regulations) which became the foundations stone of the monastic movement in the Middle Ages. (pp. 102–103)

Benedict was not a jolly sort of guy. He outlawed jokes, had an especial distaste for what he called "murmuring," and outlawed "idle talk." As a matter of fact, Benedict finally decreed that it was better not to speak at all unless given permission by someone in charge. And the abbots could own no private property.

The rules really weren't that strict. Monks had a special diet (no meat). And if they went outside the monastery, they couldn't talk about what they'd seen when they got back. Monks were well-fed and well-rested, and I have a suspicion that the occasional joke worked its way into the monastery. (As for the funny bald-on-top haircut, it was a symbol of devotion. Slaves had their heads shaved in the same way, so that they could be identified. Thus, the monks were making a statement that they were slaves to God's will.)

It was Benedict's vision of the monastery that would spread throughout Western Europe (for the most part—Ireland, as usual, is a different story). Jones goes on to say:

> For the next half millennium, Benedict's Rule was disseminated throughout the monasteries of western Europe—first under aegis of Pope Gregory the Great and then under Charlemagne. By the eleventh century his form of monasticism had a virtual monopoly of religious houses. (p. 104)

This was the birth of the monastery, and the monks and nuns of these institutions would use their powers of literacy to keep the intellectual knowledge necessary for complexity written down over the next several centuries, until the printing press allowed this knowledge to be disseminated. Already, the monastery held the seeds of its own downfall, as many institutions do, but it was to play a large part in our present conversation about Europe.

DOT 4: CHARLEMAGNE

Although the Christian church held power in the West, it was *spiritual* power, mental in nature. The pope could, for example, pass decrees about how people *should* act, but then it was up to the people whether to obey or not. The pope claimed the power to excommunicate people from the Church, effectively assuring them a place in Hell after their death, but this threat worked differently on different people. Better to have a single sword in this world than the threat of a thousand swords in the next.

What the pope needed was a military. In his biography, *Charlemagne*, Derek Wilson describes the pope's dilemma:

> Amid the splendors of the classical past, a coterie of old patrician families clung to power, and it was they who provided the Latin Church with most of its popes. By the end of the eighth century the Bishop of Rome headed an organization that administered wide estates and claimed primacy over the whole Christian world in matters spiritual. This was universally accepted throughout the churches of the West—in theory. In fact, the ability of the popes to intervene effectively in the affairs of kings and bishops in regions far from Rome was limited. Even

in Italy their position was far from secure, for what they lacked was any military muscles, and to the north lay an ever-present threat—the Lombards. These Germanic people had ruled subalpine Italy since the mid-sixth century and were ambitious to extend their control southward. By religion they had been Arians until the late seventh century, which meant they bore no allegiance to the pope and were doubly abhorrent to Rome. Successive popes were obliged to look far afield for a protector from these heretics. What they needed was a loyal son of the Church who had the backing of a strong army. The only practicable candidate was the king of the tall, red-haired barbarians who ruled Gaul. (p. 8)

Gaul was the province in which Caesar had made his military reputation. It was, at this time, the home of the Franks (the land is mostly modern France), which was the most powerful of the "barbarian" tribes in the West. Their leader was Charlemagne. The pope, threatened by Germanic Arian barbarian heretics, needed him.

It all began with Charlemagne's grandfather, Charles Martel. It was Martel, standing bravely with his troops, who turned back the Muslim advance into Europe at the Battle of Tours. (Actually, it was Odo of Aquitaine who handed the Muslims their most important defeat, but he had lousy historians and Martel had good ones.) Martel became known as the "Hammer of the Saracens." Martel's son, Pepin the Short, continued the glory of the family name by uniting many of the northern tribes and pronouncing himself king. Still, this was not a united kingdom. Wilson continues:

> What appears on historical textbook maps as "Francia" was in reality no more than a conglomeration of semiautonomous kingdoms, dukedoms and tributary states, which had emerged from the encounter of Germanic tribes with the declining Roman Empire. By far the fiercest of the barbarian settler were the Franks—tall, redheaded warriors who struck terror into the hearts of Romano-Gauls and rival invaders alike. They established their mastery in two main areas, the "East Kingdom" of Austrasia between the middle Rhine and the Moselle, and the "West Kingdom" of Neustria, which stretched southward from the Rhine estuary to the Loire Valley. (p. 6)

There was little holding these provinces together. As J. M. Roberts writes: "Europe was formed in a hostile, heathen world."

The thing about Charlemagne was, he was a true believer in Christianity. A full convert who grew up in a land that had been fiercely loyal to the pope since King Clovis had converted Gaul to Christianity in 496.

In 768, Pepin the Short, Charlemagne's father, died. Charlemagne's actions afterward are described by Wilson:

> Charles found himself joint ruler of Francia with his brother, Carloman, and there was an inevitable clash of interests and ambitions. But Carloman died at the age of twenty, leaving two infant sons to inherit his

lands. Charles grabbed the opportunity to reveal himself as a determined and ruthless king. He proclaimed himself sole ruler and forced
his brother's family into exile. . . . There were enemies within and
without his realm and he would spend almost all the ensuing forty-two
years fighting them. (p. 5)

So, here was Charlemagne: Six feet four inches tall, bearded and power-
fully built, ruthless, militantly Catholic, illiterate, and to the pope's mind,
useful.

After years of successful military conquests, Charlemagne was invited
to Rome. He arrived in November of 800. A month later, on Christmas
Day, the pope bade Charlemagne to the basilica of St. Peter. Charlemagne's first biographer, Einhard, wrote that Charlemagne had no idea
what was to happen next. Furthermore, if he had, he wouldn't have gone.

In the church on this day, the pope laid a crown on the tall Frank and
declared him king of the Romans. There was much pomp about the affair,
and the gist of the ceremony was that while Charlemagne controlled the
empire, the pope was to control him. No one at the time, other than a few
pretenders to the throne, thought much about the crowning. Historians
however, attribute significance to the event, probably because it was recorded and easy to look back on. Also, it provides historians with a rare
chance to be witty. Charlemagne was now the emperor of the Holy Roman Empire. However, as Voltaire said, and as historians love to repeat,
Charlemagne's kingdom was neither holy, nor Roman, nor an empire.

No matter. Charlemagne was king and he was Catholic, and he was
ready to bring a new force to the world. Wilson writes:

Any leader who comes with armed support in the name of a compel-
ling faith is sure of a following. The faith that underpinned Charlemagne's reign, and that would become the most power the world has
ever seen, was militant Christianity. (p. 6)

Although he couldn't read, Charlemagne's favorite book was St. Augustine's *City of God*. It was Augustine who came up with the idea that
nonbelievers imperil believers because they might bring about God's
wrath. Charlemagne took this idea to heart and had both the power and
the will to forcibly convert his enemies. Cantor writes:

[L]ike Augustine [Charlemagne] perceived the world as divided into
the saved and the damned, the good and the bad. He battled the Sax-
ons for more than thirty years. At one point, having 4,000 free men
killed to punish a revolt, he finally imposed conversion to Christianity
as a condition of peace. (p. 110)

But Charlemagne was far from a mindless barbarian warrior. He was
deeply interested in ideas and Christianity. Simply put, Charlemagne
wanted to create a Christian empire, and he recognized the importance of
learning and scholarship to attain this end. Wilson continues:

[T]he revival of classical studies and the educational reforms that Charles set in hand were not ends in themselves but must be seen in the light of his desire to establish a Christian empire. The copying and dissemination of books, the establishing of schools and the encouraging of a better understanding of Latin were all elements of a crusade to produce a corpus of clergy who could preach, properly administer the sacraments and staff the imperial administration. (p. 114)

Also:

The one area of cultural activity that comes closest to being designated as "renaissance" was book production. It followed from Charles' passion for learning that scholars needed texts to study. It was to meet the urgent and extensive needs of the palace school, and the other schools around the empire, that he had his agents scour libraries in order to borrow almost any manuscripts of interest that they could find, and his scriptorium was kept busy copying them. They were then distributed to various monasteries, especially those of the royal foundation. In this way the works of Virgil and Horace, Pliny, Livy and Seneca, Martial, Juvenal and Terrence were among those preserved for posterity. The greatest cultural debt that later ages owe to Charlemagne is the rescuing of many classical texts that would otherwise have been lost to us. The extent of that indebtedness can be numerically expressed. From CE 0 to CE 800 some 1,800 manuscripts and fragments survive. From the following 100 years we have more than 7,000. (pp. 119–120)

Charlemagne would hold together a thinly joined empire, set a precedent of spreading Christianity by the sword, and, most importantly, put the full force of his power behind the monasteries. He was a man of the sword who appreciated the power of the pen. Charlemagne's son, Louis the Pius, would use his friendship with St. Benedict to spread the formation of a uniform type of monastery, with a consistent code. Power in the Holy Roman Empire would switch to Germany, first under the reign of Otto the Great, for about two centuries, but would remain within the Carolingian dynasty. All the while, manuscripts flowed into the monasteries, where ideas leapt into the minds of eager monks in the scriptoriums.

Once freed from libraries, that information would do some incredible things.

DOT 5: MONASTIC DISCOVERIES

In *How the Irish Saved Civilization*, Thomas Cahill points out that the Irish Christians, converted originally by St. Patrick, began to move throughout the far western part of Eurasia during the early medieval period:

[W]hat is certain is that the White Martyrs [early Irish monks] clothed like druids in distinctive white wool robes, fanned out cheerfully

across Europe, founding monasteries that would become in time the
cities of Lumieges, Auxerre, Laon, Luxeuil. . . . Suffice it to say that as
late as 870 Heric of Auxerre can still exclaim in his Life of Saint Germa-
nus: "Almost all of Ireland, despising the sea, is migrating to our shores
with a herd of philosophers!" (pp. 194–195)

With the Irish monasteries spreading from west to east, and the Benedictine monasteries coming the other way (and eventually consuming most
of the Irish monasteries), soon Western Europe was dotted with these
institutions. Then, something interesting began to happen. The churches
and monasteries began to take the place of the Roman Empire. Burke
(2007) wrote:

The network of communications that maintained contact between one
part of this patchwork quilt of territories and another was that of the
Church. By the fifth century the diocesan organization of the ecclesias-
tical hierarchy corresponded to the concentrations of civil population.
When the legions withdrew, the administration of the area fell into the
hands of the bishops and their clergy: they could read and write and
the new rulers could not. For this reason the Church was granted many
privileges, in particular exemption from taxes, that helped it to survive,
while the Church itself exacted a tax of one-tenth (a tithe) from its own
tenants. By the eighth century Europe was scattered with churches and
monasteries, many of which had to provide a service that no one civil
community could have done, in the absence of a centralized power:
they ran the mails. A new church or monastery was called upon to
provide pack horses or messengers, and in some cases a freight service
of wagons, within a radius of up to 150 miles from the church. It would
seem that the Church had a bishop-to-bishop communications network
that continued to operate through the Dark Ages, connecting one kingdom with another, carrying news and information as well as ecclesias-
tical business, and transmitting knowledge in the form of copies of
manuscripts. (p. 85)

DOT 6: COPY CATS

The monks spent most of their time writing out ancient texts by hand
onto parchment. A single Bible, written on parchment, took two or three
hundred calfskins or sheepskins to make. Not only that, but turning the
skins into parchment took lots of time and money.

Once the skins were prepared, the monks began the process of labori-
ously and carefully copying, by hand, texts onto the skins, often complete
with elaborate pictures. In his famous novel, *The Name of the Rose*, Umber-
to Ecco has set his story in an abbey in 1327. This passage describes what
the working space of the monks in the scriptorium must have looked like:

Each desk had everything required for illuminating and copying: ink-horns, fine quills which some monks were sharpening with a thin knife, pumice stone for smoothing the parchment, rulers for drawing the lines that the writing would follow. Next to each scribe, or at the top of the sloping desk, there was a lectern, on which the codex to be copied was placed, the page covered by a sheet with a cut-out window which framed the line being copied at that moment. And some had inks of gold and various colors. . . . (p. 80)

What were they copying? Ecco describes this in a fascinating passage:

William bent over the lists inscribed in the codex. I looked, too, and we found titles of books we had never before heard of, and others most famous, that the library possessed.

De Pentagono Salomnis, Arsloqeundi et intelliegendi in lingua hebraica, *Derebus metallicis*, by Roger of Hereford, *Algebra* by Al-Kuwarizmi, translated into Latin by Robertus Anglicus, the *Punic of Silius Italicus*, the *Gestafrancorum* by Rabanus Maurus, and [more]. . . . (p. 83)

The monks were copying the great works from the Hellenistic and Islamic worlds into Latin, which was the language of education in the European world. The elite scholars were delving into these works, not for the purpose of finding anything they could build on, but simply to preserve the information.

Then, they started finding things.

MONASTIC INVENTIONS

Dot 1: The Clock

The Benedictine monks would also give to the world the invention that would probably have the most impact on the daily lives of more people than any other in the history of the world: the mechanical clock. Benedictine monasteries were places of strict ritual, and St. Benedict had decreed that the monks were to perform certain types of activities at specific times of the day. Burke (2007) explained that:

These hours, associated with prayer and ritual, he called "canonical" hours. The saying of prayers at the right time was part of the discipline Benedict imposed on his Order, and was essential for the monks' salvation. During the day, the canonical hours could be determined easily, with a sundial, but at night they required a member of the community to sit up all night and ring the bell to wake the others at the right time. The drive to find an automated timekeeper must have been strong. The first chronicled evidence we have that the Church was using some semi-automatic device to tell the time comes from a monk called Jocelyn de Brakelond, who wrote, among other things, about the fire in the great church at Bury St Edmunds in Suffolk on 23 June 1198. The church was a center of pilgrimage as it was supposed to house the body of the saint, and a fire was a potential disaster—both spiritually and financially—for the community. On the night in question the monks were awakened by the crackle of flames, and, in Jocelyn's words, "We all of us ran together and found the flames raging beyond belief and embracing the whole refectory and reaching up nearly to the beams of the church. So the young men among us ran to get water, some to the well and others *to the clock*. . . ." (my italics). The reason they put fires out with clocks is that the clocks were water-powered. (p. 128)

According to Burke, the water clock was known as the *clepsydra* (Greek for "water stealer"). It was probably invented in Egypt, was used by the Arabs, and then found a home in Europe, where it was useful because cloudy days rendered sundials inefficient. The water clock is sort of complicated to explain but really cool looking. Simply put, water fell out of a bucket or drain at a certain measurable rate and lifted a pointer attached to a buoyant ball. The pointer pointed at numbers 1–12 that had been set up beside it. Clever.

There were some problems though. The clock froze in the cold European winters, and the length of the days was not uniform due to the changing of seasons. The monks needed a better clock. Also, there was a new curiosity springing up in the minds of many learned people in Europe. The monks, steeped in traditions both religious and scholarly, wanted to know more about how God's universe worked, so that they could bring that sacred fire of knowledge to humanity. "What kind of clock did God have?" they seemed to be asking.

Soon enough, the monks developed a *mechanical* clock based on something called the "verge and foliot" system. I'll not go into the details for a number of reasons, not the least of which is I have no idea how it works, but this type of clock was effective. This device, originally intended to inform monks of their appointed prayer hours, soon spread like wildfire. By the end of the 13th century, the clock was used in church towers. It had no hands or face, but was used only to make lots of noise when it was time to pray.

It must have been hard to ignore the big noisy things. Astronomers noticed them and built clock faces that used the power of this new mechanism to keep the date. Burke wrote:

The earliest of these appears to have taken the form of a large face on which the pointer showed the signs of the zodiac, while windows showed other parts of the mechanism rotating the phases of the moon, the position of the sun, the major constellations as they rose and set, and certain dates, principally those of the feast days. The last was the most important function of the new clock, since the Church had a considerable number of feast days whose date depended on astronomical data. (p. 131)

Feast days were of importance not just to priests and monks but to the average worker, who also found the clock useful. What have we here? Suddenly, everybody in the town could look at the big clock in the center square and decide "We'll meet at this bell at this place," which is a much more direct statement than "We'll meet when the sun is slightly slanted in the east." Also, employers could now say, "Be here at this time" rather than "Be here at dawn." Dawn was changeable; this new idea of time was not. It was a massive change in the way that people thought of time.

Now, time was not a fluid thing, changing with the seasons, stretching and shrinking. It was *separate* from nature, hard, quantifiable, divided up into bits, ripped away from the universe and imprisoned inside a ringing monstrosity made up of gears and mechanical genius.

The Europeans now had a passion for quantification. A clock, you see, is really a specialized knife. It slices time up into units called *quanta* and then measures them out in the same way that we measure space. Have you ever really looked at a clock? It's just a ruler bent into a circle, with hours instead of inches.

The clock may be the very first piece of technology to influence the marketplace in a way that we now take for granted. When it first hit the market, it was brand new, huge, and expensive. As it spread, it got more elaborate, cheaper, and eventually much smaller. Originally a giant machine that sat in the center of town, in just a few centuries it would be wrapped comfortably around a man's wrist.

Originally, the clocks were incredibly expensive, but every little burgh felt as if it had to have one. Crosby writes:

> Every big city and many smaller ones taxed themselves severely in order to have at least one clock, which in their first century or so were huge, usually sat in towers, and were very expensive. It may be that no complicated machine in the entire history of technology before the seventeenth century spread so rapidly as the clock. (p. 84)

A clock in Medieval Europe is like a cell phone now; to say that it told the time hardly described its entire function. Crosby continues:

> Some of the most spectacular clocks ever made were constructed within the first few generations after the invention of the escapement [a piece of technology that made the clock more accurate]. The famous Strasbourg clock, begun in 1352 and finished two years later, told the hours and included an automated astrolabe, a perpetual calendar, a carillon that played hymns, statues of the Virgin with Christ Child and three worshiping Magi, a mechanical rooster that crowed and flapped its wings, and a tablet showing the correlation between the zodiac and the parts of the body, indicating the proper times for bloodletting. To say that a city's clock told time and to say no more would be like saying a cathedral's stained-glass windows admitted light and saying no more. (p. 85)

It wasn't just time that Europeans were quantifying (one might say *imprisoning*); the Europeans were just confident enough to think that it was possible to stretch space until it was all out of whack, just to suit their sailing needs. It was and they did.

Dot 2: The Map and Space

The division of space (not outer space, but just plain old space) came much more slowly to Europeans than did the measure of time. And it was not the monks who would spur on this measurement this time, but the other great staple of European civilization: sea trade.

Sailors needed some way to quantify space on a map. With the new compass, it was possible to know in what direction one was sailing but not necessarily how far one had to sail. Crosby explains:

> The first useful maps in Western Europe for laying compass courses were called *portolani*. The earliest dated example that has survived was drawn in 1296, in those same wondrous few decades in which the first clock was built. The *portolani* . . . were utilitarian drawings of coastlines with the waters, adjacent and between, scored with rhumbs (compass courses) traced with straightedge. A navigator consulting a *portolani* often found rhumbs already drawn from major port to major port, often the course he wanted. If not, he could often find a rhumb parallel to the one he needed, and he could then take his heading from that.
>
> The *portolani* were devised for enclosed or nearly enclosed waters, like the Mediterranean, the Bay of Biscay, and the North and Baltic Seas. For these they served their purpose well because they were reasonably accurate and the distances between landfalls were short. Distortions, inevitable because no one knew about compass deviation and unavoidable because the *portolani* were geometrically naïve flat pictures of the curved surface of the earth, were insignificant. But these charts were dangerously illusory over long distances. Oceanic sailors needed maps that would enable them to set courses across the surface of the planet as depicted on geometrically rigorous charts. The next stride in cartography would be toward taking the measure of area and shape, in addition to direction and distance. (p. 97)

That's a somewhat wordy way of saying that mapmakers had a way of representing real space on a map just as long as the body of water wasn't *too* big and had shores on all sides. To go farther—say, across an ocean— some new thinking was going to be required.

As was often the case in this era of European history, that new thinking came from an old source. Crosby relates that in 1400 a copy of the book *Geographica*, by the great Greek thinker Ptolemy, arrived in Florence, fresh from the not-yet-fallen city of Constantinople. From there, it went west into the rich naval centers of Western Europe and Africa.

The problem with the maps of the day was that they lacked a certain kind of thinking. They were just flattened globes, basically. An accurate representation of the Earth can't be made by just taking a mallet to a globe because that distorts the distances. To get where you're going, you've got to mess around with the landmarks a little. Crosby describes what Ptolemy had done so long ago:

> Ptolemy's contribution to cartography was, put simply, to treat the earth's surface as neutral space by slapping a gridwork on it, a cross-hatch of coordinates calculated in accordance with the positions of heavenly bodies. He provided fifteenth-century Europe with three different methods, mathematically consistent, by which the curved surface of the earth could be represented on flat maps with the unavoidable distortions managed in ways for which the informed could make allowances. By the next century Ptolemy's techniques were part of the common currency of Western European mapmakers. Their earth was now a sphere caught in a network of latitudes and longitudes, its theoretical surface as uniform as that of a billiard ball. When the Americas and the Pacific burst into Western perception, the means to depict them already existed. (p. 98)

In other words, Ptolemy had created the concept of *latitude*. To make a map that will accurately get you across the ocean, it is necessary to stretch the size of landmarks, especially at the poles, so that by sailing west or east across an imaginary straight line, a sailor can actually get to where that line is aiming. It's enormously useful for sailing. The creation of longitude, a fascinating story in its own right, occurs later in the book.

For now, let's look at another gift from the East, perhaps the gift that finally completed and confirmed the new European mathematical mindset: numbers.

Dot 3: Arabic (Indian) Numerals

It was becoming apparent to the Europeans that *everything* could be measured: Time, weight, space could all be represented mathematically and geometrically. Crosby states that:

> Certain Western Europeans of the late Middle Ages and Renaissance began tentatively to consider the possibilities of absolute time and space. The advantages were that absolute properties, by definition, were permanent and universal, which meant that it was worth the effort to measure them and to analyze and manipulate the measurements in various ways. Measurement is numbers, and the manipulation of numbers is mathematics. (p. 109)

In their passion to measure, to quantify, the Europeans were held back by the very tools of mathematics, the numbers themselves. Most of Europe had been part of the fallen Roman Empire, which meant that those people had adopted those horribly outdated Roman numerals that weren't much good for anything other than measuring out military squadrons. The Romans cared little for doodads. They cared about war, with words in the senate and weapons on the field, and mathematics was useful only insofar as it advanced Roman engineering on the lands they had conquered.

Roman numerals just weren't good enough tools for the new type of thinking that was required in Europe. The answer came—wait for it—from the East. Crosby writes:

> Little is clear about the origin of what we usually call Arabic numerals except that the Arabs did not invent them. They got them from the Hindus, who may be their inventors, but it is just as possible that the Indians got them from the Chinese. . . . Whatever the truth about their origin, the Arabs, who knew a good thing when they saw it, adopted and adapted them to their own ends. The Muslim whose name is most closely associated with the new system is the scholar and author Abu Jafar Muhammedibn Musa al-Khwarismi, who lived in the ninth century. His book on the new numbers traveled west to Spain, and the new system soon percolated into Europe. In the twelfth century an Englishman, Robert of Chester, translated al-Khwarizmi's book into Latin, and after that the influence of the new numerals to the West was continuous. (p. 112)

The numbers Crosby is talking about are the familiar 0–9, and they were accompanied by a decimal system. Suddenly, Europe got a huge upgrade in its mathematical tools. Still, it took a long time for Europe to adapt to them. The Roman numeral system of mathematics wasn't entirely junked until 1514. And that darn zero, which was a representation of *nothing*, was a difficult concept for mathematicians to grasp, especially when numbers were placed after it, representing what exactly? Pieces of nothing? Zero is nothing, but if you add a zero to the end of a one, you've increased it by 10? If you multiply a 1 by a zero then you've destroyed the one, or any other number for that matter? Strange.

So, it took a long time for the Arabic numeral system to overtake the Roman, but it happened by 1600. What those numbers did then was allow for accurate banking, which was important, since Europe was awash with gold by then. As always, more on that later. Suffice it to say that Europe was the beneficiary of so much from the East and that, gradually, as these ideas enriched Europe, her inhabitants literally came to be *of a different mind*.

Dot 4: The Cam Shaft

The Romans were very good engineers, and one of their scholars, Vitruvius, wrote about a gearing system in the year 14 CE. The gears could be used for a waterwheel, but rarely were, possibly because in the Roman world slaves did the work and none of the elite cared much about creating technology to make that work easier or more efficient.

However, in Europe of the Middle Ages, the waterwheel began to play a serious role. Between the fifth and tenth centuries, the geared waterwheel spread all over Europe to be used in grain mills, which ground up wheat so that it could be made into flour and thence bread. As Burke (2007) points out:

> In most cases such owners were churchmen, since it was they who had the knowledge to construct the mills, and the literacy to work out accounting systems to run them as businesses. . . . The Saxon word for aristocrat is "lord" meaning "loaf giver." (pp. 86–87)

At first, these mills were built basically on the blueprints that Vitruvius had written out. The monks who copied the Roman's plans were not trained to think that these plans could be *improved* upon. (By the way, do you see how the monks, since they have the rare talent of literacy, are getting rich?) However, in the ninth century, something happened. Burke writes:

> [I]n the ninth century a breakthrough occurred. . . . It may even have been that a monk came across the idea in a manuscript he was translating from Greek. The device first appears in Switzerland, and probably originated somewhere in the Alps. The first reference to it appears in CE 890 in the monastery of St. Gall, where it was being used to make beer for the monks. The device in question was the cam, a Hellenistic invention dating from the second or third century before Christ. In its simplest form it is a piece of wood set on the side of a shaft, so that as the shaft turns, the protruding piece of wood strikes against anything placed in its way. The coupling of the cam with the waterwheel gave Europe the power source it needed almost exactly at the right time, as the Viking invasions to the north and the Arab incursions to the south began to tail off. (pp. 88–89)

We could do well to remember Archimedes who fought off the Romans in Sicily, only to be killed while drawing mathematical equations in the sand? The ideas from that world were not all lost, but simply were locked up in books, waiting to be able to leap from the page and into someone's mind. When those books were finally opened—by monks—the ideas leapt out, ready to *do* something.

What the cam shaft did was immediately combine with another idea that came after it in the Roman world, that of the grinding wheel. Combined, they made something incredibly complex. But the cam wasn't done. Burke continues:

> What followed between the tenth and fourteenth centuries has come to be known as the Medieval Industrial Revolution. The cam was used in various ways: to trip a hammer every time it rotated to its original position, to push down the end of a lever and activate a suction pump at the other end for raising water from wells, or to act on a crank to turn the rotary motion into horizontal back-and-forward motion for operat-

ing knives or saws. The beer-making mill at St Gall used the hammer, to crush malt for beer. A hundred years later, in CE 990, there were hemp mills in southern France, hammering rotted flax stalks or hemp to knock out the fibers in preparation for the making of cord or linen. By the eleventh century there were forge hammers in Bavaria, oil and silk mills in Italy; by the twelfth century there were sugar-cane crushers in Sicily, tanning mills pounding leather in France, water-powered grinding stones for sharpening and polishing arms in Normandy, ore-crushing mills in Austria. From then on the use of water power spread to almost every conceivable craft: lathes, wire-making, coin-producing, metal-slitting, sawmills and—perhaps most important of all—Liege, northern France, in 1348 the first water-powered bellows providing the draught for a blast furnace. (p. 89)

Dot 5: European Fashion

After Genghis Khan's death in 1224, the empire he'd connected created new demand for consumer goods. When Mongol influence reached Europe, European fashions changed. Weatherford writes that:

> In addition to new forms of fighting, new machines, and new foods, even the most mundane aspects of daily life changed as the Europeans switched to Mongol fabrics, wearing pants and jackets instead of tunics and robes. . . . (p. xxiv)

Tunics and robes, pants and jackets all were made in the monasteries, where textile (clothing) production took place because of, you guessed it, the cam. Burke (2007) writes:

> [I]f the recovery of Europe owed its success to any one particular variant of the waterwheel and cam, it was to its use in the textile industry, in the form of fulling mills. These used the trip hammer to pound alum and other astringent materials needed to clean and take the grease out of newly woven cloth, and then to pound the cloth itself so as to soften and intermix the fibers, giving it a "fuller" appearance. By the thirteenth century, fulling mills were turning out ever-increasing amounts of cloth in northern Italy, Flanders, along the banks of the Rhine in Germany, and in England. And the source of their raw material—wool—was the same as that of the technology itself had been: the monks, and in particular, an order known as the Cistercians. (p. 89)

The wealth of the Benedictine monasteries had upset a monk named Robert of Molesme, who lived in France. In 1098, he broke away from the Benedictines and set up a new type of monastery in the Citeaux forest, hence the name *Cistercian*. These houses spread quickly and became almost like medieval factories, churning out textiles and making a fortune.

The monks couldn't seem to buy the poverty they claimed to crave.

Dot 6: New Plow

Not all of the new inventions in Europe can be attributed to the monasteries. In the sixth century, a new type of plow came to Europe, although we don't know from where. Up to this point, the Europeans had been using the old-fashioned "scratch" plow, not much different from the kind used by ancient Egyptians.

The new plow was called a *mouldboard plow,* and it was innovative in a number of ways. Burke (2007) writes:

> The plow has wheels on the front, so that it could easily be taken from field to field. The major innovation lies in the way the plow cuts. On the frame ahead of the share is a knife, placed vertically to cut the sod and make it easier for the share to enter the thick soil. Behind the share is a curved, wing-like board, sitting diagonally to the frame, to lift the cut sod and throw it clear to the right, like a wave breaking. This was the mouldboard, and it may be said that this single fitting was the main cause of the agricultural revolution that was to follow, since it permitted land to be plowed at its wettest. It did make a U-turn at the end of the field, and then return to make a furrow parallel with the first, going in the opposite direction. The result was a series of ridges and furrows, with the highest point of the ridges at the center of the field, running like a kind of spine down the center of the plowed area. This allowed the water in the field to drain off to the sides. (p. 63)

Burke then points out that this new plow was heavy and had to be pulled by oxen. The bigger ones required eight oxen to be pulled! No peasant could afford this, so they had to pool their resources and began to live in villages. Land was divided up differently, into rectangles rather than squares, because it was better to cut long furrows. The serfs began to cut their new fields into the forests. And the plow was not finished; it was just a piece of complexity. It was now going to combine with other inventions.

Dot 7: Adding to the Plow—The Harness and Horseshoe

The horse is extremely significant in world history. A large animal, relatively easy to tame, able to sweat and run long distances, able to be ridden and harnessed, the horse gave a distinct advantage to whatever society possessed it. However, when the mouldboard plow was invented, it had to be pulled by ox. An ox could be harnessed to a plow with bands that went across the animal's belly and neck. This harness would quickly strangle a long-necked horse.

Clearly, there would have to be a new type of harness used if "horse power" was to become a factor in plowing. Burke writes:

> The horse collar, which was put to use in front of the plow some time in the eighth or ninth century may have originated in Bactria in the sixth

century as a form of harness for camels. Whether it came to Europe north from the Arabs, or south from the Vikings (some of whom had seen service in the Byzantine Empire and may have brought the idea back with them) is not known, but by the tenth or eleventh century the new harness was firmly established. It made an immediate difference, for the horse can work twice as much land as the ox. Production increased as a result and therefore so did the population. (p. 65)

The horse collar allowed for *twice* the agricultural production as the ox harness. Now, Europe's population began to explode, with some unfortunate consequences. By the eleventh century, the horseshoe was being used in Europe, which allowed for horse travel in rough terrain. As travel became easier, people could live farther away from their fields and places of work, since it was now possible to commute. This caused villages to grow even larger.

Dot 8: Crop Rotation and the Musical Fruit

The plow created its own problems for Europe. There was more food, but there were also more people and more animals to feed. For centuries, in Europe, farmers would grow crops in one field and let their animals graze and defecate in another field. That gave the soil a chance to recover, and the animal waste fertilized it. Soon enough though, the Europeans moved to a three-field system. They'd grow beans and peas in the spring, cereal crops (wheat and barley mostly) in the fall, and leave a third field empty or fallow. Legumes (beans—sort of, all beans are legumes but not all legumes are beans) can perform a neat trick. They take nitrogen from the air and fertilize themselves and the soil they grow in at the same time. Beans are also high in protein, which was something missing from the carbohydrate-rich diet of the peasants. Burke (2007) explains that:

> With the combination of carbohydrates from cereals, fats from animals, and the 50 percent increase in output from the three-field system, the population of Europe took off. The way people lived began to change very much for the better. (p. 66)

At this point, we can see that the European "barbarians" who had been so looked down upon by the civilized peoples of the East were beginning to stir in a big way. All of those inventions from the East were finding in Europe an idea workshop, where inventions already created were combining in a burst of ingenuity.

ASSESSMENT

In his book, *Measuring Reality*, Alfred Crosby (1997) wrote of Western European mathematics during the Medieval era:

Mathematics was not ready for swift advance. Its symbols and techniques were inadequate. The moment had arrived for a trumpet solo, and the only instrument available was a hunting horn. (pp. 110–111)

Explain how technology had advanced European civilization, and why a paradigm shift in mathematics was necessary for Europeans to leave the mindset of the Middle Ages behind.

TEN

Lesson Four: Caffeine and Connections—A Tempest in a Coffeepot

A simple graphic drawn on a chalkboard could illustrate the purpose of this lesson. Imagine a board with the word "coffeehouse" in the center and then a list of different regions from Latin America, West Africa, Europe, the Middle East, and North America placed in a ring around the center. The coffeehouse affected each of these regions, intertwining them into a system of global trade.

This lesson begins by inviting students to draw connections between the coffeehouse to see the big picture, by involving them in a deep lesson for how one region, Latin America, was transformed by the trade, and then requiring students to engage in the same process themselves after the teacher has modeled the way in which research produces a narrative. Once students have studied the coffeehouse and Latin America's transformation, they can engage in researching the way in which the global trade affected other regions of the world.

Some of the historical reading can be dense and, to hear students state it, occasionally boring (there are, to date, no boy wizards or vampire romances featured in Latin American history) but teachers are not entertainers. Students must stretch their attention spans to meet the requirements of the teacher, not the other way around.

For students, the era of economic globalization that began after 1492 can be dizzying. European ships spun webs of trade between the Americas, Europe, and Africa, giving birth to a global economy that was unequal from the outset.

This global economy, spawned by European economic demand for sugar, coffee, and liquor, developed rapidly into a machine driven by

93

coercive labor. The southern hemisphere, with its tropical climate, largely supplied raw materials to the northern hemisphere, which used them to industrialize. This relationship between supply, demand, and labor set the economic foundations for the future.

There are many ways in which to begin and shape a lesson such as this one. A teacher could have students read an article about the way in which poverty afflicts Haiti and much of South America and contrast this with the standard of living in the United States. This may generate questions that could be answered through historical analysis.

Students might also be invited to compare activities that occur in modern coffeehouses with those that took place in Enlightenment-era establishments that served the same beverage. This helps to draw connections between the past and present in a way that highlights similarities.

FROM FRISKY GOATS TO THE ENLIGHTENMENT: DEMAND

Dot 1: Goats and Beans

After Columbus, the world was interconnected in a way that had never been seen before. It can be difficult to keep track of all that was happening during this tumultuous era, so it helps to find something that interconnects all of these historical developments. That common ground (yes, that's a pun) can be found through a study of the coffeehouse, through which all of the varying aspects of global history of the era can be processed.

It seems that the Enlightenment owes a large debt to frisky goats. Coffee, "the second most valuable exported legal commodity on earth (after oil)" likely has its origins in what is now modern-day Ethiopia.

The traditional story of where coffee comes from (the story that appears on the Starbucks website as well) involves an Ethiopian sheepherder who noticed that his goats were dancing and bleating joyfully after having eaten red berries from an unknown bush.

Thinking that maybe the goats were onto something, the boy decided to try the berries the next day and, sure enough, found that the berries made him dance as well. People talked (as they will if you dance with goats), and soon word about the powerful cherries got around. The coffee cherries were probably used in a number of ways at first: possibly rolled up with animal fat to make the world's first power bars—or power balls, if you prefer—or used to make a kind of tea.

The first written record that we have about coffee comes from the 10th century, when an Arab doctor named Rhazes wrote about it. Coffee as we know and love it was probably not created until the 16th century, when the beans were roasted and ground. Before that, people drank something called *quishr*, which was a kind of wine made from the fermented pulp of the coffee cherry.

Immediately, coffee and conversation became tied together. Ethiopian coffee drinkers still sit and chat while charcoals in a pot heat up, the coffee beans are roasted, stirred, and ground, and the grounds boiled into coffee. The conversation, of course, goes on while the coffee is being drunk, in the same way it has for centuries.

Dot 2: Into the Arab World: The Birth of the Coffeehouse

Both coffee, and the conversation that it inspired, diffused to the Arab world, where the Arabs seemed to have enthusiastically taken to both the drink and the talk. It was the Arabs who gave coffee its name. They called it *qahwa*, which is Arabic for "wine" and the world, like Al-jabr, evolved to fit European tongues.

Coffee had a religious purpose, in that Arab Sufi monks used it to stay up for midnight prayers. It was, like sugar, considered by some to have medicinal properties. Soon enough (as sugar would in Europe), coffee came to be a symbol of status. Wealthy people had entire rooms built just for the drinking of coffee.

And it is here, in the Arab world, that the coffeehouse was born. Not everyone could afford a coffee room, so *kavehkanes*, coffeehouses, were built so that even the poor could imbibe. From its very inception, the coffeehouse was a place where social rank mattered little; hence, it was one of the few places where hierarchies fell apart and ideas could easily spread (Pendergrast 1999).

Of course, there was also a little mischief brewing in the coffeehouses. Gambling and other illegal activities were fairly common. Most interestingly, coffeehouse conversations often became subversive. The governor of Mecca, Khair-Beg, was upset to find that he was being made fun of by some of the patrons of the Meccan coffee establishments. He searched in vain for a prohibition against coffee in the Koran ("If liquor was against Koranic law, then this stupid drink must be too!" he must have thought). Despite his inability to find a specific law banning coffee, he managed to twist the arms of the religious authorities and, in 1511, he became the first political figure to shut down the coffeehouse.

The ban did not last long. The little bean had friends in high places, and the sultan of Cairo overruled Khair-Beg. Later, the Arab governor of Constantinople shut down coffeehouses there for precisely the same reasons that Khair-Beg had. One could be beaten for drinking coffee at that time (coffee has its own martyrs), and yet coffee and ideas percolated underground until the ban was finally lifted.

Despite its controversial beginnings, coffee was absorbed deeply into the culture of Turkish society. The coffeehouse became an important place for Turks to gather for a variety of reasons: for conducting business, talking politics and religion, reading poetry, or just exchanging ideas. Apparently, a woman could divorce her husband if he did not supply her with enough coffee.

Eventually, coffee beans were cultivated in the southern Arabian Peninsula, once the Turks took over Yemen in 1536. It was, in a way, the Arab version of Chinese silk. Both were in high demand in Europe, and the secrets to how both were made were closely guarded. In the 17th century, a few coffee beans were smuggled to India and, by 1699, the Dutch, who stood atop a burgeoning maritime trade empire at the time, were soon growing trees in Indonesia, on the island of—you guessed it— Java. Sumatra soon followed, and then the island of soymilkmachioto (kidding).

Dot 3: Europeans and Coffee: Scientific Revolutions and Coffee-Inspired Revelations

European travelers to the Ottoman Empire began to write about coffee in the early 17th century. One European writer, George Sandys, noted that the Turks loved coffee and conversation, but he also noted that the viscous Turkish coffee had the effect of a laxative.

Pope Clement VIII had been told that coffee, this drink so beloved by the Muslims, was "Satan's drink." However, the pope soon changed his mind. In Italy, coffee then acted pretty much as any other commodity does on a capitalist market, which was then just beginning to flower in Europe due to the copious amounts of gold and silver that were flowing in from South America (more on that shortly). Coffee started out as a drink for the wealthy, and then, over the course of a few decades, became a staple of life for the lower classes. The exception was in France, where, like a lot of things in Paris, it enjoyed a short and trendy run among the fashionable class. (The French medical community also noted that coffee had a desirable effect on the bowels. Freshmen and Frenchmen appreciate such details for some reason.)

It was in France that the powerful Turkish coffee was ameliorated. The French took coffee with milk and, soon enough, seemed to be taking their milk with coffee. The result was the famous *café au lait* that is just now becoming so popular with Americans.

England really became the center of coffeehouse life. It is possible that the scientific tempest of the 17th century formed in a coffeepot. The coffeehouse produced a culture of its own. Unlike the rowdy bars of Europe, the coffeehouse was a place where intellectuals could meet, read the newspaper, and converse without being put into a headlock by a longshoreman. In his book *The Forgotten Genius: The Biography of Robert Hooke 1635–1703*, Stephen Inwood (2006) writes of the coffeehouse's rapid spread:

London's first coffee house, Pasqua Rosee's Head, opened in St Michael's Alley, off Cornhill, in 1652, on a site later occupied by the Jamaica Wine House. Coffee houses sold exotic and increasingly popular commodities, including Arabian coffee, West Indies sugar, Virginian tobacco, Chinese tea and South American cocoa, and they offered comfortable, lively and relaxed meeting places which suited to perfection the needs of middling Londoners (rich enough to spend a few pence a night, but too poor to entertain lavishly at home). When licensing was introduced in 1663 there were eighty-two in London, and by . . . 1703 there were at least 500, perhaps many more. (p. 142)

I can't help but quote from Neal Stephenson's epic work of science fiction, *Quicksilver* (2003). In this scene, the main character, Dr. Daniel Waterhouse, encounters his first cup of coffee. "The first sip had been tooth-looseningly unpleasant, like one of those exotic poisons that certain Royal Society members liked to brew. But he was startled to notice after a while that the cup was empty."

In short order, Dr. Waterhouse found himself jerking about excitedly, "[H]e got into a shin kicking match with his own table and produced a disturbance that sheared cups off their saucers. Everyone looked" (p. 87).

The great scientist and author of *Micrographia*, Robert Hooke himself spent a good deal of time in coffeehouses, chatting with other "natural philosophers" and imbibing a good bit of caffeine. There's no evidence, however, that he ever got into a kicking match with a table, although it's certain he would have liked to have kicked Isaac Newton.

Hooke loved to converse over caffeine. "Coffee Houses, most of all Garraway's, were Hooke's favourite places for meeting friends and craftsmen, and for picking up, showing off, and passing on pieces of scientific and mechanical information."

Dot 4: 1683 Siege of Vienna

The coffeehouse is not just a good vehicle for understanding economics; a good deal of conventional history can be studied through its movements as well. One of the great historical narratives of the 17th century involves Europe's cultural, military, and scientific rise above the Arab/Muslim world that had dominated and threatened the West for so long.

In 1683, the Ottoman Turkish empire began a clear decline in terms of power against the West. In this year, the Ottomans laid siege to Vienna under the direction of Sultan Mehmed IV, who decided to start a military campaign against the Austrian Hapsburgs. By July 14, the Ottomans sat outside the city walls of Vienna with a huge army made up mostly of stragglers (Pagden 2005). The Austrian nobility had already escaped, but they need not have. Soon enough, the siege of Vienna was neatly broken up by a pan-European force of about 60,000, led by the Polish king, John Sobieski. It was a history-altering defeat for the Muslims. "Mehmed's failure was to be the very first step in the steady but inexorable decline of what had for so long seemed, to Christian and Muslim alike, the unstoppable advance of the Ottoman Empire. After Vienna, the relationship between Christendom and Islam began to change" (Pagden 2005, p. 285).

Indeed it did. This decisive victory is a key event in the history of both East and West, and, rightly so, historians have long focused on the implications of this pan-European military victory. (A string of Ottoman military failures would follow.) It is unfortunate that the smell of gunpowder overpowered the smell of a freshly brewed pot of coffee because it was after this battle that the coffee bean came to Austria to stay. The Ottomans had been in such a rush to get away that they left a good many supplies behind. After the battle, Franz George Kolschitzky found a bag of coffee. As an ambassador to the Arab world, he knew what the beans were and how to use them. He later opened the Blue Bottle, which was the first coffeehouse in Vienna. Coffee became a raging smash hit (as drugs tend to do) among Viennese artists. Anyone who has listened to Beethoven would probably not be surprised to learn that he was a hardcore coffee addict, as was the famous French author Balzac, who sounds like he'd had a couple of cups in this quote about the effects of coffee: "Everything becomes agitated. Ideas quick march into motion like battalions of a grand army to its legendary fighting ground, and the battle rages. Memories charge in, bright flags on high; the cavalry of metaphor deploys with a magnificent gallop."

Dot 5: Revolutionary Conversations

Not only did coffee stimulate the mind, but the coffeehouse became a place where caffeine-infused people, regardless of class, could talk. This is from the diary of one educated Londoner, James Boswell:

> We are fortunate enough to have records of actual conversations which went on in coffee houses. James Boswell . . . enjoyed the coffee houses of London as a young Scot trying to make his way in the world of English capital. His favourite haunt was Child's Coffee Shop in the Strand. . . . Reading the papers or drinking tea and coffee could be as easily undertaken here as in any other coffee or tea shop. What drew Boswell to it, however, was the conversation. Child's was "quite a place to my mind, dusky, comfortable and warm, with a society of citizens and physicians, who talk politics very fully and are very sagacious and sometimes jocular." (Outram 2006, p. 65)

Dare it be suggested that the coffeehouse was the place where revolutionary ideas transferred from the elites to the masses?

The coffeehouse was where true egalitarianism took place. One Italian visitor to a coffeehouse stated that the houses were places "where one can hear everything that is believed to be new, be it true or false; and in two hours 'one pays only for what one has drunk'" (Outram 2006, p. 65).

According to David Hume, Europe was experiencing an economic revolution that set the foundations for conversation. Awash in luxury goods (Europe was going through a capitalist revolution), Europeans of a certain social class were free to enjoy things and talk. "Hume knew that ideas cannot be passed sociably without a certain form and direction of economy, and that people have little incentive to come together without it. Luxury and civility lead straight to inquiry" (Outram, 2006, p. 66).

In other words, people came for the coffee, and once there, stayed for the conversation. Sometimes, those conversations were dangerous to the authorities.

All over Europe, people sat over their cups of hot coffee, chocolate, and tea, perhaps puffing on a pipe or cigar, blew steam off their drinks, and did what people do when grouped together: they talked. Most of it was inconsequential gossip, about the weather or about mutual friends. Some of it, however, was revolutionary. In these coffeehouses, ideas, coming from the lips of caffeinated speakers, began bouncing frantically around.

A free exchange of ideas is dangerous for those who seek to control minds. When people began to talk about political revolution, rulers got nervous. In 1675 and into 1676, English King Charles II tried to shut the coffeehouses down for the same reason that the governor of Mecca had: They had become places where people made fun of their political betters and gossiped about their rulers. Charles stated that coffeehouses should be "put down and suppressed" because "in such houses divers false malitious and scandalous reports are devised and spread abroad to the Defamation of His majesty's Government and to the Disturbance of Peace and Quiet of the Realm" (Inwood, 2003, p. 211).

The ban lasted only six months. The people could deal with public executions, oppressive regimes, and corrupt tax collectors. Taking away their daily cup of coffee, however, proved to be too much to bear.

Dot 6: The First Global Marketplace

Fashionable coffeehouses were the first places where goods grown halfway across the world could be bought and sold cheaply by the masses and were, thus, the first truly global marketplaces. Coffeehouses were also the first establishments to expand like the modern corporate franchise, in which each house owned by a particular individual or corporation was similar to the next.

The story of the coffeehouse is symbiotic with the rich history of sugar. Sugar was in high demand, especially because of its ability to sweeten bitter drinks. Sidney Mintz has written the authoritative book on the topic of the sugar trade and its place in world and American history, *Sweetness and Power: The Place of Sugar in Modern History*.

In the book, Mintz details that sugar was used to make wine, gin, and other alcoholic beverages. These drinks were widely consumed in the American colonies. When temperance movements arose in the colonies and Europe, tea was used as a suitable alcoholic substitute. Tea was advertised as being the beverage that "cheers without inebriating" (Mintz 1985, p. 137).

Tea and coffee, being bitter by nature, were sweetened with sugar. So, whether a colonist or European was drinking alcohol or not, he or she was likely using a large quantity of sugar throughout the year. Alcoholic drinks were never supplanted by tea or hot chocolate, so the combined consumption of both led to an extremely high demand for sugar in the colonies and Europe. (The upper classes of Europe especially consumed copious amounts of sugar. Mintz's book includes recreations of huge decorative confectionary houses that were put on display during parties for the rich and the nobility.)

The coffeehouse is also the best example of the emerging global marketplace that had been growing since 1492. The European coffeehouse depended, in fact, upon goods that were being supplied from diverse places around the world. "The sociable Enlightenment was sustained, in its turn, by the growth of global trade. Tea and coffee came from India and the Americas, chocolate from South America, sugar from the Caribbean. Books were traded internationally" (Outram 2006, p. 62).

Economics plays by certain rules, the most basic of which states that if a product is in demand, then it must be supplied. Interestingly, for geographic determinists, hot drinks were being chugged in the generally cool climate of Europe, where coffee, tea, and sugar won't grow. These items were supplied by the south, where the climate allows for such growth. So, let's look at those areas supplying the coffee, sugar, and other commodities that were in such high demand in European coffeehouses. Oddly and irrevocably, the people of the southern hemisphere were finding that their lives had become intertwined with the demands of Europeans.

Dot 7: Teacher-Led Modeling: The Coffee Trade's Effects on Latin America

Historians typically divide Latin American history until the early nineteenth century into stages, those being: pre-Columbian, conquest and settlement, and independence. The dramatic arrival of Columbus in 1492 turned the Caribbean into a massive biological experiment as plants, animals, and diseases from two long-separate continents suddenly mixed together. "The Columbian Exchange," as it was termed by Alfred Crosby, drastically altered the physical and economic makeup of the regions involved.

After Europeans arrived, South America and Europe would both be drastically altered. Europe's population surged forward, thanks in large part to the nutritious Peruvian potato, while South America's population declined. South American culture was, in some senses, erased and then redrawn by European settlement. The native populations that survived their "discovery" would continue to rebel, but the Europeans had come to stay and to colonize this resource rich land, and this process of colonization followed certain patterns. Most of South America's transformation can be studied through the history of the coffeehouse, since the gold and silver from the continent transformed Europe's economy, giving common people wealth and leisure for the first time — which they spent in coffeehouses — and creating a demand for the coffee and sugar that fueled these hangouts.

After the era of conquest, the Spanish established cities in South America so that Spanish colonists could live the life of the urban elite that most had hoped to live in Spain. These cities were based upon a basic grid pattern. Much of Spanish colonial life centered around these cities. "The 'urban nucleus' . . . became fundamental to the pattern of Spanish imperialism. Nearly all the modern Spanish American republics have capital cities that can trace their history back for well over four hundred years and to their 'foundation' by a particular conquistador" (Collier, Skidmore, Blakemore 1992).

The two most important cities in Latin America were at the sites of the two most dramatic Spanish conquests. One was in Mexico, built on the Aztec city of Tenochtitlan. The other was in Peru, at the former Inca capital of Cuzco, which was in the mountains. The Spanish also needed access to sea trade, so an important city, Lima, was carved out on the Peruvian coast.

The Spaniards came to South America to get rich. The conquistadores, as we've seen, quickly absconded with an enormous amount of gold. After gold, however, it was soon realized that South America was home to impressive silver deposits. "In the early stages of colonization, gold was washed from rivers on the Caribbean islands. On the mainland, silver was the previous metal found in greatest abundance. Spectacular silver-strikes occurred around the mid-point of the sixteenth century: in 1545 at Potosi in Upper Peru (now Bolivia), in 1548 and 1558 at Zacatecas and Guanajuato in Mexico. From this time onwards, silver-mining became an important factor in consolidating settlement patterns in the Spanish American empire." Mining centers such as Potosi became significant markets, with large populations, while the need for safe and regular transport of silver to Spain helped determine major trade routes and the shape of the commercial system in general.

This gold and silver eventually shattered the European feudal system and set up Hume's luxury class. The European coffeehouse likely would have existed without South American and Caribbean sugar, but probably would not have come into being without South American gold and silver.

The Spanish seemed to like South America, but wished it was more like Spain. They also needed to find a way to put all of those surviving Native Americans to work. So, they began to transplant Spanish crops and agricultural techniques from Spain to South America.

To put the natives to work in the mines and on the plantations, the Spanish rounded up the Indians into something called the *encomienda*. The Spanish basically divvied up the human population and doled them out to work on the farms that the Spanish were building on land that had formerly belonged to the Indians. The Spanish justified this by saying that they were actually—get this—*helping* the Indians. They were, after all, saving Indian souls and bringing them civilization. Indians who escaped this system had to pay taxes.

Not everyone was happy with this system. The Spanish priest de las Casas (who owned black slaves and used to own a plantation that used the *encomendia* system) spent much of his life, which ended in 1566, arguing strongly for the rights of American Indians.

It was not until 1550, when just about everything that could be conquered was and the Taino people were almost completely gone, that the new Spanish governors outlawed a ban on further conquests.

For the Spanish, the New World consisted of a paradise of cheap land where gold and silver flowed from the ground. A Spaniard (to the dismay of the Spanish royal family) could set himself up as a virtual noble within the encomienda system. For the Indians, things were not so bright.

For the Indians, conquest and colonization meant that they were living in what seemed to be a foreign land. "Their lands, too, were steadily encroached on by the newcomers, although it was not until the seventeenth century that the great estate began to assume its place as the dominating feature of the Spanish American rural scene. . . . " (Collier, Skidmore, Blakemore 1992, p. 192).

Because the conquistadores were all men and relatively few women were coming to South America from Spain, there was, of course, a good deal of (ahem) *interaction* between Spanish men and Indian women. Inevitably, the mixed-race offspring were given a specific name. *Mestizos* came to mean a person who was half Spanish and half Indian. When African slaves flooded the region later to work on plantations, the racial mixture became even more complicated.

Spanish royalty was busy trying to create an absolutist government back home and certainly didn't want a new and powerful Spanish nobility growing just across the Atlantic, so the powers of the *encomenderos* (plantation owners) were checked by law. Spain set up a colonial government.

Vice-royalties were set up in Mexico (then called New Spain) and in Peru. Very quickly, the conquistadores, who had done the macho work of conquest, were marginalized as bureaucrats moved in to govern. "Spain's empire was to be an empire, not a patchwork of unruly territories governed by powerful warlords. (That was to come later, after independence.)" (Collier, Skidmore, Blakemore 1992, p. 193).

Due to the absolutist nature of Spanish politics, there arose a great desire among the Spanish to control the economic system in Latin America. Trade between Spain and Europe remained closely regulated and huge fleets carried raw silver from the Latin American mines back and forth between Spain and the New World. Spanish silver would eventually drift all the way to China.

Near the end of the 16th century, Spain's brand of economics, religion, and political system were well entrenched throughout nearly all of South America. Even the population had a radically different face as a generation of mestizos began to come of age.

The Spaniards and Portuguese then negotiated and decided to draw a big line on the globe at 370 leagues west of the Cape Verde Islands. Anything west of that line went to Spain; anything east to Portugal.

This was called the Treaty of Tordesillas and its signing shows, even more than the dramatic conquest of Indian peoples, the new power that Europe held. "We'll take *this* and you take *that*," the Portuguese and Spaniards were saying about the world, as if they were children dividing up a playground. The fact of the matter is that they had the power to actually divide the world up and rule it, just that easily.

In practice, the Treaty of Tordesillas meant that the Portuguese controlled Brazil, a huge chunk of eastern South America. This proved to be the most important jewel in the Portuguese crown.

"Brazil" gets her name from a type of dyewood that grows there. The wood itself was why the Portuguese wanted the area, and, for a while, it was the colony's only major money-maker. To their delight, the Portuguese found that the Indians would work for trinkets like glass and tools. Soon enough, a few Portuguese businessmen set up wood factories.

The problem was the French: They kept attacking the factories, and they had cooler trinkets to give the Indians, who often joined them in these attacks. The Portuguese didn't care too much about conquest and settlement — they wanted to trade — but they had to do something to fight off the French.

The solution to French interference was to conquer the coast and set up a new system of settlement and hereditary land passage that was watched over and granted legitimacy by Portugal's king. "This system [was] half feudal, half commercial. . . . Settlers were taken there, and both cattle rearing and sugar cultivation were introduced. . . . In Sao Vicente, there were six sugar mills and 3000 Indian slaves by 1548. In the northeast, the able soldier Duarte Albuquerque Coelho had the funds to bring in mercenaries and subjugate the Indians of Pernambuco" (Thomas, Skidmore, Blakemore 1999, p. 195).

Shortly, we'll see how quickly Brazil became a major part of the Triangular Trade, in which those sugar plantations took on extreme importance. South America had been totally altered. It was conquered, settled, and governed in a way that would make it the optimal place from which to export sugar and coffee.

For the Indians of Brazil, the story took on a sad but familiar narrative. They were captured and made slaves, or simply had their land taken and were forced deeper and deeper into the jungles. Disease, of course, devastated their numbers and inhibited their ability to fight back. They could stage the occasional surprise raid, but, by 1560, epidemics had cut their population in half.

As the Indian population dwindled, the European population in South America exploded. Increasingly, Africans arrived on the Brazilian coast and soon the populations of South America and the Caribbean began to look radically different. These are the basics of Latin American history. Now we see how the coffeehouse is intertwined with this narrative.

Interestingly enough, the history of coffee and sugar explains much of why the world's rich live in the northern hemisphere and why the poor live in the southern hemisphere.

The histories of Africa, the United States, and South America were all altered by the coffeehouse. Coffee is now produced all over the world. "That cup of coffee you sip at your breakfast table, or café comes from far away. It was grown in Brazil, Colombia, Vietnam, the Ivory Coast, or one of a hundred other coffee-producing lands on five continents. . . . There is a world of history in your cup."

Coffee is currently grown on five continents, in more than 100 countries. "Essentially poor countries have grown coffee for rich ones" (Clarence-Smith & Topik, 2003, p. 5).

Why is this?

Sugar and coffee grow best in hot climates, and the West Indies were very suitable for the growing of sugar cane. Columbus first brought sugar cane to the islands in 1493, on his second voyage, and it was one of the European crops that transplanted very well.

It's important to ask students the following question: If sugar is going to be grown in the Caribbean, then who exactly is going to harvest it and work the crop?

The answer involves making a connection to a past lesson on Columbus. Students already know that Columbus and the Spaniards had completely decimated the Taino tribes living in the West Indies. Having studied how the Spaniards depopulated the West Indies, we can then see how the islands were *repopulated* through the African slave trade, giving the area a very different type of populace. The West Indies are now populated almost entirely by people of African decent, whereas before the population was entirely "Indian."

Equally as interesting, and more often forgotten, is the huge impact that this slave trade had on Native Americans. Since Indian slaves had both a knowledge of the American terrain and a place to escape to, they were difficult to keep in slavery in the American colonies. The solution to this "problem" for slave-owners was simply to sell the Native Americans to the West Indies, to work the sugar and coffee plantations there (making escape virtually impossible). In his book *Lies My Teacher Told Me*, James Loewen (1995) points out that Charleston, South Carolina, shipped roughly 10,000 Native American slaves to the West Indies in just one year (p. 106). It is also worth noting that Oliver Cromwell, Puritan dictator of England for a time, shipped thousands of Irish, Welsh, and Scottish slaves to the West Indies to be "employed" in the sugar trade. Sugar, sold in mass quantities in coffeehouses throughout Europe and the colonies, fueled the African slave trade and drastically changed the face of the West Indies and northern South America.

Because South America was such a great place for growing the types of crops in demand in Europe and North America, we can see how the two regions entered the first phase of globalization at very different places. Africa, as well, was sharply changed by slave labor, even as many of her people drastically altered the human geography of the West Indies and South America.

The coffeehouse was where these slave-worked crops were sold and consumed. To the south, the only thing being consumed were human lives. The discontent of the slaves, and the nature of the slave trade itself, would soon guarantee this system's demise.

CONNECTING THE DOTS: THE HAITIAN SLAVE REVOLT, NAPOLEON, AND THE LOUISIANA PURCHASE

(ALL THIS OVER COFFEE?)

Many great historians have examined the causes and effects of European conquests in isolated parts of the world. Two, however, have specifically looked at the biological results of New World conquest. Jared Diamond and Alfred Crosby both note that Europeans were able to take over in areas where the latitude was similar to Europe's. Look around the globe at places like Australia, New Zealand, parts of South America, and all of North America, and you'll see that Europeans were able to push out indigenous peoples. However, arguably, the most deadly of European diseases—smallpox—didn't have much effect on central Africans. In fact, when Europeans went into central Africa, it was *they* who died rather than the indigenous peoples.

Why? Simple: The tropics are home to many diseases to which Africans had already evolved immunities. Plus, the central African tribal people were cattle herders. Smallpox comes from the cow. These people had contracted smallpox and had already evolved a certain level of immunity to it.

If disease comes from animals, as Jared Diamond, Alfred Crosby, and Norman Cantor have pointed out, then whenever a group comes into contact with a foreign animal, or someone who has been infected by a disease from a foreign animal, then that group is bound to get sick.

The central Africans also had something that the Europeans didn't: *Monkeys*. In *Guns, Germs, and Steel* Diamond points out: "The yellow fever virus is carried by African wild monkeys, whence it can always infect rural human populations in Africa, whence it was carried by the transatlantic slave trade to infect New World monkeys and people" (p. 204).

As a general rule, free labor detests slavery since slaves take away paying jobs. In the northern colonies, labor put up a strong resistance to slavery (they also opposed abolition, which would have created a rise in the northern free labor pool, thus driving down wages). In the West Indies, no such labor movement existed, largely because the area was mostly populated by Europeans, especially the French, who had no desire to do the actual work of harvesting sugar cane.

What happened was this: The market favored a type of trade system that at first seemed to perpetuate itself but, in the end, only planted the seeds of its own destruction. Here's how it worked:

1. Sugar was made in Haiti and traded to the colonies.
2. The colonies turned the sugar into rum.
3. The colonies traded rum to Africa for slaves.
4. The slaves in Africa were sent to make more sugar in Haiti.
5. More sugar meant the creation of more rum in the colonies to be traded to Africa for more slaves.
6. More slaves in Haiti meant more production of sugar.
7. And on and on.

This is, of course, the famous (among history teachers, anyway) "Triangular Trade Route." In this case, the nature of a market economy forced the sugar plantation owners to try to grow as much sugar as possible in order to meet demand. Thus, plantation owners flooded Haiti with as much slave labor as possible.

The West Indies, packed with slaves that outnumbered their masters nearly 8 to 1, would revolt in 1793. The United States, relatively fresh from her own revolution, would have to deal with a black slave republic just south of Florida. The political and ideological ramifications of the slave revolt were a major part of Adam's administration and sparked many a debate about the nature of slavery in the colonies.

The slaves in the West Indies, having come from Africa, had been in contact with the yellow fever virus, which is spread by mosquitoes, because either they or their relatives had been in contact with monkeys. As is always the case in such occurrences, an arms race occurred between the human immune system and the yellow fever virus. Over time, the Africans developed what Crosby, when speaking about European immune systems, refers to as "internal armor."

Napoleon wanted to subvert the Haitian colony for his own, but, when his troops attacked the little island in 1802, he found that the freed slaves were not only tenacious fighters but that they possessed a powerful weapon that up to that point had almost always been in favor of the Europeans: germ warfare. Napoleon's troops, having dipped south of the Tropic of Capricorn, came into a different climate, hosting different animals and diseases.

When the French showed up, a "virgin soil" epidemic was the result. Only, in this case, the people came to the contagion rather than the other way around. Napoleon left between 20,000 and 50,000 French corpses in Haiti, admitted his failure to subdue the island, and gave up his dream of a Caribbean colony. His only choice was to sell his claim to all North American French holdings to the United States, during Thomas Jefferson's term as president. This became known as the Louisiana Purchase.

The coffeehouse is a perfect nexus from which to understand many connecting and concurrent historical themes; it's a factor that cuts across economics, biology, and history. That's a lesson that should wake you up.

POST STUDY QUESTIONS FOR STUDENT RESEARCH

1. *What were the ramifications of this trade for the North American colonists?*

Possible Student Answer: It could be argued that this trade set up a pattern in which the southern hemisphere "supplied" the northern hemisphere using cheap labor. This, of course, enriched many northern countries and left the southern hemisphere in relative poverty.

In due time, the British colonists in North America became aware that they were, in fact, supplying Great Britain in the same type of subordinate relationship. The colonists were selling raw materials, such as wood and furs, to Great Britain and getting manufactured goods in return.

This method of mercantilism was relatively satisfactory to the colonists — that is, until Thomas Paine's *Common Sense* was published. The mercantile system was clearly set up to benefit the British. The colonies legally had to buy their manufactured goods from Britain. They could not buy them elsewhere nor produce them on their own (a colonial relationship that Britain would continue to impose all the way up to Gandhi's famous salt march). The colonists were further prevented from selling their raw materials on an open market. These raw materials had to be sent to Britain (*46 Pages: Thomas Paine, Common Sense, and the Turning Point to Independence*, Liell, p. 60). Such an economic system would later become incendiary to a colonial populace that was looking for a plot behind every British action. The British, in seeking to add taxes to a relationship that was already benefiting the Crown, gave the colonists further grievances.

2. What were the results of this trade for Africa?

Possible Student Answer: The Africans were tribal; they did not consider themselves "Africans." The slave trade was absolutely dependant on the nature of African tribal society. African tribes captured and enslaved other tribes, or else sold off members of their own tribe. In the process, many of these tribes became a part of the global web of capitalism and forgot how to fend for themselves. Many of these tribes became very wealthy from the capture and sale of other Africans. However, when the slave trade finally ended, West Africa was deprived of several generations of young people. Also, the warlike tribes that were left suddenly found themselves without means of employment.

3. What were the results for the West Indies?

Possible Student Answer: The West Indies, packed with slaves that outnumbered their masters nearly 8 to 1, would revolt in 1793. The United States, fresh from her own revolution, would have deal with a black slave republic just south of Florida. The political and ideological ramifications of the slave revolt were a major part of Adam's administration and sparked many a debate about the nature of slavery in the colonies. Napoleon's failed efforts to subdue the slave leader Toussaint L'Overture would cause him to give up his dream of a Caribbean colony and sell his claim to all American French holdings to the United States during Thomas Jefferson's term as president.

The French Revolution would nearly correspond with the Haitian Revolt. It seemed as if the Americans had sparked a worldwide revolt against the "old guard." Many Americans, especially Jefferson, were left with the odd prospect of supporting the revolution in France as a revolt of democracy against tyranny, while being against the same type of revolt in Haiti because it upset the supposedly "natural" order of the slave–master relationship.

ELEVEN

Lesson Five: Applications of Insights to a Historical Narrative

The following lesson requires a very high level of reading comprehension and thought, but a skilled teacher can help by slowly bringing students to an understanding of the material covered. For a lesson like this, one of the most important notions that a teacher can impart is that education can be difficult. Students have to work through difficult tasks in reading or understanding in the same way that they have to practice to succeed in any other endeavor.

This lesson repeats some concepts stated in earlier lessons, but by reading information in a different context, students can strengthen their connections to the material. The mind learns by laying threads of information, growing stronger in mastery every time.

The process for the study below is to have the students analyze and understand the two quotes from Enlightenment-era philosophers, then to read the following excerpt. The process involves (1) interpreting the quotes, (2) reading specifically to find the three impacts of technology on history, and (3) applying their understanding of the quotes to the narrative recently learned.

> Those sciences which are remote from each other cannot be extended without bringing them nearer and forming points of contact between them. (Marquis de Condorcet, 1794)

> This search and study of the history of the mind, ought not to be confined to one art only. It is by the analogy that one art bears to another, that many things are ascertained, which either were but faintly seen, or, perhaps, would not have been discovered at all, if the inventor had not received the first hints from the practices of a sister art on a similar occasion. The frequent allusion which every man who treats of any art is obliged to make to others, in order to illustrate and confirm his

principles, sufficiently show their near connection . . . . (Joshua Reynolds, 1776)

THE CONCEPT OF INTELLECTUAL GEOGRAPHY: THE THREE WAYS IN WHICH TECHNOLOGY AFFECTS SCIENCE

In the history of science, technology tends to overturn the existing order by discovering new facts that may not fit into the existing paradigm. This narrative, finally formalized by Thomas Kuhn in his 1962 classic "The Structure of Scientific Revolutions," can be summarized thus: A technological advancement evolves, followed by new evidence, followed by a crisis to the existing paradigm, and then a new paradigm emerges, which gains acceptance until a newly evolved technology begins the process again. In this vein, John Gribbin declared "What is much more important than human genius [for the development of science] is the development of technology, and it is no surprise that the start of the scientific revolution 'coincides' with the development of the telescope and the microscope" (2004, xix). Technology does affect science by collecting new information, but it also provides new problems in need of novel solutions and occasionally improves the metaphors and analogies we use to describe phenomena.

In 2012, the physics community was thrown for a (strange) loop when with the now-disputed discovery that neutrinos may travel faster than light, in a way that seemingly contradicts Einstein's theories, would seem to fit snugly into the accepted Kuhnian narrative. What is the CERN particle collider, responsible for troublesome experiments, but another meddlesome technology in the vein of Galileo's telescope? Aren't those speedy neutrinos merely doing to Einstein what the moons of Jupiter did to Aristotle's concept of a static universe? Perhaps. But this narrative about the effects of technology on science needs not revision, but addition. New technologies affect science in two ways, beyond the discovery of new evidence. First, technology provokes new problems that require novel solutions. Second, new technologies can provide theorists and thinkers with new sets of metaphors and analogies. Given recent structural changes in theoretical physics, these effects may be the more significant to the history of science and its ongoing progress than to the discovery of new facts.

Before delving into the history of technological change and its other effects on the human mind, it is necessary to define two concepts. First, imagine struggling to explain photosynthesis to a five-year-old. This would involve trying to match the complexity of photosynthesis with the comparatively uncomplicated language and sets of metaphors in her lexicon. Fifteen years later, it would be possible to explain photosynthesis to that young woman in a much more complete way. Why? The process of photosynthesis remained unchanged, but the child (now a young woman) grew up and expanded her vocabulary, set of metaphors, and analogies, and hence her understanding.

Of course, the environment in which this young woman grew up would affect her ability to understand photosynthesis. The next question would then be, for an educator, what kind of environment would best train her mind to a fuller understanding of photosynthesis? To explain this concept historically, let me (cautiously) coin a phrase based upon Jared Diamond's work *Guns, Germs, and Steel*. In that book, Diamond argued that, although human beings may be genetically equal, the geography they settled was not. Certain parts of the world—the Fertile Crescent in particular—had better foundational materials, such as wheat and animals suitable for domestication, which gave humans in those regions certain advantages over human populations who settled in regions that were less geographically suited for the creation of civilization and technological complexity.

Some parts of the world developed numbers and mathematics in order to adjust to the problems presented by civilization. This historical concept is best summarized by Thomas Jefferson, who, in 1787, wrote the following in response to two European pseudoscientists who thought Native Americans must have been racially inferior because they lacked scientists and writers:

> Before we condemn the Indians of this continent as wanting genius, we must consider that letters have not yet been introduced among them. Were we to compare them in their present state with Europeans North of the Alps, when the Roman arms and arts first crossed those mountains, the comparison would be unequal, because, at that time, those parts of Europe were swarming with numbers; because numbers produce emulation, and multiply the chances of improvement, and one improvement begets another.

To summarize Jefferson's point, it was as absurd to fault Native Americans for a lack of genius as it would be to fault Midwesterners for lacking championship level surfers. In fact, a *Skeptic* article by Stephen Sniderman noted that serendipity often creates the right conditions to groom certain types of athletes. Often, certain racial components are correlated with those athletes, but this does not make certain racial groups superior at any one sport. The same is true for intellectual development, and, as Jefferson stated, once the culture has enough intellectual tools (letters and numbers) to create a certain threshold, "one improvement begets another."

It is now possible to look at the role of technological evolution in enriching that concept by creating an environment that provides a new set of analogies to be used and by presenting new sets of problems to be solved. First, please note that the term "inventor" is a poor one and should be replaced with "selector." Technologies evolve, and the people who help them do so are analogous to an environmental factor in biology. Edison, for example, no more "invented" the lightbulb than a dog breeder invents puppies. Edison mixed technological DNA together until he got the product he wanted, therefore acting as a kind of domesticator of a process of technological evolution that had, for a long time, been subject to the laws of randomness.

Diamond's thesis about the importance of geography for world history would note that civilization had a head start in the Fertile Crescent because this region had the best grains and animals. The pressures of civilization then created an intellectual geography, first in Sumer, then elsewhere, which required record keeping for the purposes of keeping track of economic transactions. A rudimentary set of written symbols evolved to meet these new needs. Once those symbols became available, other uses were discovered for them, and soon enough they were used for the creation of epic tales like *Gilgamesh*.

In India, where the numbering system was shaped by Hinduism's concept of nirvana and eternity, Hindus thought about time on a large scale. Such contemplations very likely led Hindu thinkers to develop the numbers 1 through 9 (and, around 500 CE, the all-important 0), and those numbers, of course, turned out to be equally as useful for calculating the circumference of the Earth or working out the heliocentricity of the solar system as they were for reaching a state of oneness with the universe.

This narrative need not be detoured by the movements and effects of 0–9, but it is important to note that Europe produced no Galileos or Newtons until after 0–9 displaced the rusty Roman numeral system and thus provided an intellectual geography in which mathematicians could flourish.

The point being that the physical geography of Eurasia, by providing the necessary environment for the development of civilization, in turn produced new problems and analogies that enriched the intellectual geography. Originally, each civilization developed in its own separate historical Petri dish, but through trade and conquest (beginning with Sargon of Akkad, then following with Alexander, Rome, the Muslims, and the Mongol Khanate), those civilizations made contact and shared their ideas and technologies.

Envision one of those wall posters where a large picture (usually of Yoda or some other idol to geekdom) is actually made up of an amalgam of smaller pictures. Or, think of the so-called Cambrian explosion, when simple organisms finally reached a point at which their biological traits could either combine with other traits for a new purpose, or turn out to have a new purpose in a new environment.

Eurasia proved to be the place where the actual geography, settled on an East–West axis, provided the conditions by which technology could spread and synthesize, thereby enriching the intellectual environment by creating both new problems and analogies. To use but two examples, gunpowder created problems that required novel solutions, and the clock influenced the development of capitalism, biology, theology, and physics.

Edward Gibbon, fascinated and slightly repulsed by the rapid development of gunpowder technologies in Christian and Muslim lands between the 13th and 15th centuries wrote:

> By the Venetians, the use of gunpowder was communicated without reproach to the sultans of Egypt and Persia, their allies against the Ottoman power; the secret was soon propagated to the extremities of Asia; and the advantage of the European was confined to his easy victories over the savages of the new world. If we contrast the rapid progress of this mischievous discovery with the slow and laborious advances of reason, science, and the arts of peace, a philosopher, according to his temper, will laugh or weep at the folly of mankind. (p. 1168)

For all of Gibbon's considerable genius, he was quite wrong to imply that reason and science progressed despite gunpowder's evolution. Science and reason progressed *because* of it. The Chinese discovered the recipe for gunpowder earlier than anyone, but the intellectual geography of China did not provide the right types of pressures for its further development, as Jack Lindsay noted: "Since the Chinese used their techniques and recipes in this field [gunpowder technology] for fireworks, we see that they lacked the war pressures, the continual experimentation with fire-missiles, which were driving the Byzantines and Westerners on (1974, p. 370).

I should pause to note that the Chinese also first developed block printing, but, infamously could not take advantage of it because of a long and cumbersome alphabet. Only when the technology reached Germany (and a phonetic alphabet) did it flourish. One might wonder why this process did not first occur in the Muslim world, closer to China. The answer is that the intellectual geography there had turned dangerously conservative. Scribes did not want to lose their jobs and, in 1515, on the penalty of death, the Ottoman sultan banned the new technology when it first appeared in Turkish lands.

Gunpowder technology was released from China by the Mongols, who in the mid-13th century invaded Europe, crushing Russia, but getting stalled in Hungary due to succession problems when their khan, Ogodei, died. The Mongols therefore left gunpowder on the European doorstep, rang the doorbell, and then ran away. By 1249, in an eerie passage, the Franciscan monk Roger Bacon recorded the earliest known European reference to gunpowder when he wrote down the recipe and noted "and so you will make thunder and lightning."

Europeans were in the best position to benefit from gunpowder because the Christians who lived there possessed the knowledge of how to make church bells. Of course, if one flips a church bell over and fills it with gunpowder, one gets a new weapon. Edmund Burke noted that "the first cannons—called *bombards*—were paradoxically made by craftsmen who had for several centuries been associated with the doctrine of peace: they were bell-founders" (p. 69).

Europe, therefore, became the primary beneficiary of gunpowder technology. Now, any good historian, no doubt, would protest this thesis and with good reason. After all, the three Muslim empires to the east— the Ottoman, Safavid, and Moghul, respectively—have attained the title of "gunpowder empires." The Ottomans, especially, flourished by using gunpowder technology. How can it be said that Europe was the primary beneficiary?

The answer is that gunpowder's largest influence on Europe was not military, but intellectual. The Ottomans never produced what Alfred Crosby calls a new class of military technological specialists. He noted that the "Turks . . . drew their gunpowder gurus from the Balkans, Italy, and elsewhere in Europe" (2002, p. 120). The most famous of these gurus was a disgruntled cannon-maker named Urban, who sold his cannon to Sultan Mehmet II, who used them to help bring down Constantinople in 1453.

Here's the thing, though: The Turks were buying the fruits of European intellectual labor and therefore failed to develop the mathematical techniques that evolved to handle the logistical problems provided by the new ballistics. In contemporary terms, this would be analogous to the United States buying all of its nuclear weapons from India, thus allowing Indian scientists to develop the techniques in physics that would, in time, turn out to have other uses.

In Europe, mathematicians who tried to aim cannon balls had to create new mathematical forms, most of which disregarded Aristotle's flawed concepts of motion, in order to deal with the new problems posed by cannon fire. It turns out that if one develops the mathematics necessary to describe the way in which small spheres move in relation to gravity, then one has created an intellectual geography by which some other bright spot might apply the same concepts to the way that really big spheres (say, planets) move in relation to gravity. Or, as Jack Lindsay wrote, "by the mid-fourteenth century there was pressing need to grapple with the ballistical problems raised by the new exploding force . . . the key pressures leading to Galileo and Newton came from the sphere of war, from ballistics" (1974, p. 383).

Galileo and Newton, geniuses to be sure, had the luck to grow up in an intellectual environment enriched by mathematical concepts developed as a result of serendipitous technological evolution.

One other way in which technology influences science is by providing analogies for the description of the universe. With this in mind, it is fair to say that the technology that has most influenced science is neither the telescope nor the microscope, but the clock. The clock as we know it likely evolved from the sundial. It eventually became a water clock, which worked by having water drip from a top bucket into a bottom bucket, where it raised a buoyant ball with a pointer.

The pointer pointed at the numbers 1–12 that had been set beside it. The water clock seems to have made its way to Europe as a gift from the Abassid caliph in Iraq to the great Charlemagne (whose intellectual curiosity garners too little attention from historians). Later on, Benedictine monks, whose lifestyle was based upon strict prayer times and provided unique environmental pressures, adopted the water clock. Edmund Burke wrote that "During the day, the canonical hours could be determined easily, with a sundial, but at night they required a member of the community to sit up all night and ring the bell to wake the others at the right time. The drive to find an automated timekeeper must have been strong" (p. 128).

The water clock, which operates just fine in Iraq, did not do as well in France, where most of the monasteries were located. The French winters tended to freeze time. The physical geography and climate of Europe, once again, provided the right conditions for a technological development that would enrich the intellectual geography.

Somehow, a mechanical clock evolved in this environment (probably by borrowing gear technology already employed in mills) and, by the end of the 13th century, the clock appeared in church towers. Soon enough, every town featured one of these ringing monstrosities. Some historians argue that the invention of the clock spurred capitalism by encouraging set working times not based on the ever-changing length of day and by contributing to the notion that laborers should be paid by the hour.

George Lakoff and Mark Johnson (1980) even argue that the clock–capitalism connection has so influenced our thinking that we continually equate time, which we spend, save, and waste, with money. Alfred Crosby (1997) posits that the clock grew out of a sudden European passion for quantification, in which time was cut up into quanta just like distance, which is why clocks look so much like rulers bent into circles. Of course, this brings up another question: If rulers measure space, then what does a clock measure?

(The best answer is that a clock measures movement, which is interesting because, prior to the Big Bang, there was no movement, and therefore, no time. So, the Big Bang was not an event in time and cannot be understood as a dot on a timeline.)

The most important effect of the clock, perhaps, is that it provided a new analogy for the universe, one exploited by Newton, who imagined a universe that worked by certain consistent and observable rules, just like a clock. This concept leaped (as scientific concepts too often do) into the realm of mysticism and religion, where the concept of God as a disinterested clock maker became known as Deism.

Then, in the 19th century, William Paley used a small version of a clock—a watch—to construct the mother of false analogies. He stated that if one comes across a watch, then one must assume there is a watchmaker. Darwin, who famously stayed in Paley's old dorm at Cambridge, wrestled with this analogy until his discoveries in the Galapagos provided him with a better analogy. The clock was not created; it evolved. Paley had only a supposition, whereas Darwin could produce evidence.

Clocks are not made out of nowhere by people with no previous technologies, as one would expect from Paley's analogy. Instead, they evolve over time, with humans acting as environmental selectors. In a debate over whether a clock (or any other technology) evolved or was created, the Darwinist will be able to present a long evolutionary bush of ancestors dating back to the sundial.

Einstein's insight involved linking time and space in such a way that time only appears to be moving at the same rate for human beings because we all move at roughly the same speed. His calculations showed that no absolute time exists, but rather, that time fluctuates depending upon the speed that one was moving, something beyond the experience of humans.

The clock, then, having randomly evolved in Western Europe, enriched the intellectual geography and influenced the economy, biology, and physics in ways that have shaped the scientific mind ever since. The clock, because of its complexity, provided an important metaphor for theorists and allowed thinkers existing in the intellectual geography of Europe to come to a deeper understanding of the universe than those who could only contemplate the universe using less complex analogies.

This brings us to the final point about the supposed finding of faster-than-light neutrinos. Einstein also began his Theory of Relativity with the presupposition that the speed of light is the only constant in the universe, and that if this can be taken as a solid syllogistic base (always a problem for philosophers), then the ensuing equations would explain much of the way that the universe behaves.

This did not mean that nothing can go faster than light any more than the assumption that the universe works like a clock discounts the existence of phenomena that acts in a non-clocklike way. The CERN particle collider, even if it does not exhibit the existence of faster-than-light particles, will no doubt uncover facts that will fall outside of existing scientific understanding. Physicists steeped in the history of their field will be neither surprised nor upset by this.

However, the CERN collider may turn out to have a more important use for physics than the discovery of particles. It may provide new problems that will require innovative forms of thought to solve, or, more importantly, a readily available metaphor that can be used by physicists. I know of one analogy already. In his book about the CERN Large Hadron Collider (LHC), Amir Aczel wrote:

> One of the interesting things about the LHC and its construction is that no one really knows the properties, peculiarities, strengths, and weaknesses of this colossal creature. . . . And because it was put together in components by several different teams of scientists and engineers, its various parts have different personalities that need to be trained to work together (2010, p. 52).

A massive construct put together in pieces by hyper-intelligent people, each an expert in his or her own specific area, but with almost no one sure of how the construct works in its entirety? This sure sounds like the entire edifice of theoretical physics.

Conclusion: A Vision for the Future

In April 2011, my toddler son, Ben, was diagnosed with a brain tumor called ependymoma. His subsequent treatment began with a tumor removal surgery so complicated that it staggers the mind, followed up by radiation treatment so precise that it targeted only the tumor bed, leaving his cognition and personality intact. As of this writing, Ben is in remission, and my wife and I considered him cured. That is, cured with a period, not with an exclamation point but not really with a question mark either.

Just a few decades ago, the success rate in the treatment of these types of tumors remained dismal. The surgery was nearly impossible to perform and subsequent radiation therapy, necessary to prevent a recurrence, destroyed the cognitive function of children under three. Groups of dedicated professionals, working to shape a field and build upon each other's findings, developed better surgical techniques for tumor removal.

Physicist and radiation oncologists, unsatisfied with the way in which radiation treatment damaged healthy brains, built upon knowledge to overcome seemingly impossible problems in radiation physics to create new techniques for treating tumor beds. Professionals from the fields of neurosurgery, physics, and oncology all worked together toward a common goal and shared their findings through conferences and research journals.

This combination of determination, intelligence, and cooperation saved my son's life. He runs around today, pestering his brother, learning words, and cuddling with his parents because people who treat pediatric tumors refused to be defeated by the obstacles confronting them and treated the matter of pediatric tumors with the appropriate urgency.

This type of approach can also be applied to improving secondary teaching. By defining teaching as a field, experimenting with techniques, and defining our profession, teachers can overcome many of the immense obstacles before us.

A journal (or series of journals) dedicated to the publication of practical examples by teachers who have embraced the curricular philosophy expounded here would provide new teachers not only with a ready assemblage of lessons, but invite them to engage in a process. The field of teaching can be redefined using the history and philosophy of science as a guide while incorporating information from the newer fields of neuroscience, mind, brain, and education (MBE), and even theoretical physics.

Potential critics of this philosophy will, no doubt, state that teachers do not have time to engage in the processes called for here. This is invalid, since teachers coach sports, direct plays, and sponsor clubs all while managing classrooms. For education to improve, teachers really should not be pulled in so many different directions, lest the classroom experience of their students suffer. Besides, this book represents a call for teachers to achieve greatness. Professors, brain surgeons, and accomplished artists become successful by immersing themselves in a field of endeavor and making it part of their daily lives. Successful educators should do so as well, and we need not wait on anyone to dictate the terms; instead, we can simply embrace a new philosophy and change our profession from the classroom out.

References

CHAPTER 1

Gribbin, John (2004). *The Scientists: A History of Science Told Through the Lives of Its Greatest Inventors*. New York: Random House.

Kramnick, Isaac (Ed.). 1995. *The Portable Enlightenment Reader*. New York: Penguin Books.

Watson, Peter (2010). *The German Genius: Europe's Third Renaissance, the Second Scientific Revolution, and the Twentieth Century*. New York: HarperCollins.

CHAPTER 2

Bain, Ken (2004). *What the Best College Teachers Do*. Cambridge, United States: Harvard University Press.

Bain, Robert (2010). "I Gotta *Learn* All That Stuff?" "Well, I Have to Teach It All!": Managing the laments of world history teachers. *Social Studies Review* 1: 30–37.

Burke, James (2007). *Connections: From Ptolemy's Astrolabe to the Discovery of Electricity: How Inventions Are Linked—and How They Cause Change Throughout History*. New York: Simon & Schuster.

Carretero, M. (1994). Historical knowledge: Cognitive and instructional implications. In M. Carretero & J. Voss (Eds.), *Cognitive and Instructional Processes in History and the Social Sciences* (pp. 357–376). Hillsdale, NJ: Lawrence Erlbaum Associates.

Darling-Hammond, Linda (2010). They're number one: Finland came from behind to become the world leader in student achievement. Their strategy is the opposite of what we're doing in America. *NEA Today*, 29, 30–36.

Freedman, Sarah Warshauer (2001). Teacher research and professional development: Purposeful planning or serendipity? In Ann Lieberman & Lynne Miller (Eds.), *Teachers Caught in the Action: Professional Development That Matters* (pp. 188–208). New York: Teachers College Press.

Gordon, Stephen P. (2004). *Professional Development for School Improvement: Empowering Learning Communities*. Boston: Pearson.

Jarvis, Peter (2010). *Adult Education and Lifelong Learning: Theory and Practice*. London, England: Routledge.

Loewen, James (1995). *Lies My Teacher Told Me: Everything Your American History Textbook Got Wrong*. New York, United States: Simon & Schuster.

Maxim, George W. (2010). *Dynamic Social Studies for Constructivist Classrooms: Inspiring Tomorrow's Social Scientists*. Boston: Pearson.

Schweikart, Larry & Allen, Michael (2007). *A Patriot's History of the United States: From Columbus's Great Discovery to the War on Terror*. New York, United States: Sentinel.

Sergiovanni, Thomas J. (2005). *Strengthening the Heartbeat: Leading and Learning* San Francisco: Jossey Bass.

Trilling, Bernie and Fadel, Charles (2009). *21st Century Skills: Learning for Life in Our Times*. San Francisco, United States: Jossey-Bass.

Troman, G. & Woods, P. (2001). *Primary Teachers' Stress*. New York: Routledge/Falmer.

Wilson, N.J. (2005). *History in Crisis? Recent Directions in Historiography.* Upper Saddle River, NJ: Pearson Prentice Hall.

CHAPTER 3

Gessen, Masha (2009). *Perfect Rigor: A Genius + The Mathematical Breakthrough of the Century.* Boston: Houghton Mifflin Harcourt.

Gleick, James (2011). *The Information: A Theory, a Flood.* New York: Pantheon Books.

Gribbin, John (2004). *The Scientists: A History of Science Told Through the Lives of Its Greatest Inventors.* New York: Random House.

Kuhn, Thomas (1996). *The Structure of Scientific Revolutions* (3rd ed.). Chicago: The University of Chicago Press.

Shermer, Michael (2011). *The Believing Brain: From Ghosts and Gods to Politics and Conspiracies: How We Construct Beliefs and Reinforce Them as Truths.* New York: Times Books.

Snyder, Laura J. (2011). *The Philosophical Breakfast Club: Four Remarkable Friends Who Transformed Science and Changed the World.* New York: Broadway Books.

Watson, Peter (2010). *The German Genius: Europe's Third Renaissance, the Second Scientific Revolution, and the Twentieth Century.* New York: HarperCollins.

Wilson, Edward O. (1998). *Consilience: The Unity of Knowledge.* New York: Vintage Books.

CHAPTER 4

Brooks, David (2012). *The Social Animal: The Hidden Sources of Love, Character, and Achievement.* New York: Random House.

Cattell, J. (1886). The time taken up by cerebral operations." *Mind*, 11, 277–282, 524–538.

Dewey, John (1910). *How We Think.* New York: Barnes & Noble.

Dewey, John (1899). *The School and Society.* New York: Barnes & Noble.

Dewey, John (1902). *The Child and Curriculum.* New York: Barnes & Noble.

Gladwell, Malcolm (2008). *Outliers: The Story of Success.* New York: Back Bay Books.

Hebb, D. (1949). *The Organization of Behavior.* New York: Wiley.

Samuels, B. M. (2009). Can differences between education and neuroscience be overcome by mind, brain, and education? *Mind, Brain, and Education*, 3(1), 45–53.

Simon, Herbert A. (2001). Learning to research about learning. In M. Sharon Carver & David Klahr (Eds.), *Cognition and Instruction: Twenty-five Years of Progress.* Mahwah, NJ: Lawrence Erlbaum Associates.

Stanovich, K. E. & Cunningham, A. E. (1993). Where does knowledge come from? Specific associations between print exposure and information acquisition. *Journal of Educational Psychology*, 85.

Tokuhama-Espinosa, Tracey. (2011). *Mind, Brain, and Education Science: A Comprehensive Guide to the New Brain-Based Teaching.* New York: W. W. Norton.

Willingham, Daniel T. (2009). *Why Don't Students Like School: A Cognitive Scientist Answers Questions about How the Mind Works and What It Means for the Classroom.* New York: Jossey Bass.

Wolfe, Patricia. (2001). *Brain Matters: Translating Research into Classroom Practice.* Alexandria: Association for Supervision and Curriculum Development.

CHAPTER 5

Crowther, F., Kagaan, S. S., Ferguson, M., & Hann, L. (2002). *Developing Teacher Leaders: How Teacher Leadership Enhances School Success.* Thousand Oaks, CA: Corwin Press.

Darling-Hammond, L. & Sykes, G. (Eds.) (1999). *Teaching as the Learning Profession: Handbook of Policy and Practice.* San Francisco: Jossey-Bass.

Darling-Hammond, Linda (2010). They're number one: Finland came from behind to become the world leader in student achievement. Their strategy is the opposite of what we're doing in America. *NEA Today, 29,* 30–36.

Hord, S. M. (2004). *Learning Together, Leading Together: Changing Schools through Professional Learning Communities.* New York: Teachers College Press.

Oser, F. K. & Baeriswyl, F. J. (2001). Choreographies of teaching: Bridging instruction to learning. In V. Richardson (Ed.), *Handbook of Research on Teaching* (pp. 1031–1065). Washington, DC: American Educational Research Association.

Payne, Ruby K. (1996). *A Framework for Understanding Poverty.* Highlands, TX: Aha! Process.

CHAPTER 6

Mlodinow, Leonard (2008). *The Drunkard's Walk: How Randomness Rules Our Lives.* New York: Vintage Books.

Stewart, Ian (2010). Behind the scenes: The hidden mathematics that rules our world." In David Brooks (Ed.) *Seeing Further: The Story of Science, Discovery, & the Genius of the Royal* Society London: HarperPress.

CHAPTER 7

Chin, Ingfei (May 2006). Born to run.*Discover.* Retrieved from http://discovermagazine.com/2006/may/tramps-like-us/article_view?b_start:int=1&-C=

Crosby, Alfred W. (2002). *Throwing Fire: Projectile Technology through History.* Cambridge, UK: Cambridge University Press.

Diamond, Jared (1992). *The Third Chimpanzee: The Evolution and Future of the Human Animal.* New York: Harper Perennial.

Diamond, Jared (September 2005). The shape of Africa. *National Geographic.* Retrieved from http://ngm.nationalgeographic.com/ngm/0509/resources_geo2.html

Reader, John. 1997. *Africa: A Biography of the Continent.* New York: Vantage Press.

Wheeler, P. E. (1988) Stand tall and stay cool. *New Sci.* (London), 12 May.

CHAPTER 9

Burke, James (2007). *Connections: From Ptolemy's Astrolabe to the Discovery of Electricity: How Inventions Are Linked—and How They Cause Change throughout History.* New York: Simon & Schuster.

Crosby, Alfred (1997). *The Measure of Reality: Quantification and Western Society, 1250–1600.* Cambridge: Cambridge University Press.

Gribbin, John (2004). *The Scientists: A History of Science Told through the Lives of Its Greatest Inventors.* New York: Random House.

Kuhn, Thomas (1996). *The Structure of Scientific Revolutions* (3rd ed.). Chicago: The University of Chicago Press.

CHAPTER 10

Collier, Simon, Skidmore, Thomas E., & Blakemore, Harold (1992). *The Cambridge Encyclopedia of Latin America and the Caribbean*. New York: Cambridge University Press.

Inwood, Stephen (2006). *The Forgotten Genius: The Biography of Robert Hooke, 1635–1703*. San Francisco: MacAdam/Cage.

Outram, Dorinda (2006). *Panorama of the Enlightenment*. Los Angeles: Getty Publishing.

Pagden, Anthony (2009). *Worlds at War: The 2500 Year Struggle between East and West*. NY: Random House.

Pendergrast, Mark (2010). *Uncommon Grounds: The History of Coffee and How It Transformed Our World*. New York: Basic Books.

Stephenson, Neal (2003). *Quicksilver*. New York: HarperCollins.

CHAPTER 11

Aczel, Amir D. (2010). *Present at the Creation: The Story of CERN and the Large Hadron Collider*. New York: Crown Publishers.

Burke, James (2007). *Connections: From Ptolemy's Astrolabe to the Discovery of Electricity: How Inventions Are Linked—And How They Cause Change throughout History*. New York: Simon & Schuster.

Crosby, Alfred (1997). *The Measure of Reality: Quantification and Western Society, 1250–1600*. Cambridge: Cambridge University Press.

Crosby, Alfred (2002). *Throwing Fire: Projectile Technology through History*. Cambridge: Cambridge University Press.

Finkel, Caroline (2005). *Osman's Dream: The History of the Ottoman Empire*. New York: Basic Books.

Gribbin, John (2004). *The Scientists: A History of Science Told through the Lives of Its Greatest Inventors*. New York: Random House.

Jefferson, Thomas (1787). Notes on the state of Virginia. In Isaac Kramnick (Ed.), *The Portable Enlightenment Reader* (1995).

Kuhn, Thomas (1996). *The Structure of Scientific Revolutions* (3rd ed.). Chicago: The University of Chicago Press.

Lakoff, George & Johnson, Mark (1980). *Metaphors We Live By*. Chicago: The University of Chicago Press.

Lindsay, Jack (1974). *Blast Power and Ballistics: Concepts of Force and Energy in the Ancient World*. New York: Barnes and Noble.

Measurement of the neutrino velocity with the OPERA detector in the CNGS beam. 2011. Cornell University Library, September. Retrieved January 1, 2012, from http://arxiv.org/abs/1109.4897.

About the Author

Chris Edwards, EdD, is the author of two books of philosophy, one of which has been translated into Polish. He is a frequent contributor on the topics of law, logic, theoretical physics, and pyschology to the science and philosophy journals *Skeptic* and *Free Inquiry*. His original "connect-the-dots" teaching methodology has been published by the National Council for Social Studies. A ten-year veteran of the classroom, he proudly teaches world history and Advanced Placement world history at a public high school in Indiana.